THE
REAL MAN'S
COOKBOOK

MARK MacINTYRE

ROBERTSBRIDGE
SEVERN

THE
REAL MAN'S
COOKBOOK

MARK MacINTYRE

edited by
MARGARET GORE

ROBERTSBRIDGE SEVERN
in
association with
CENTURY PUBLISHING

To my Mother, who taught me ``take no prisoners''
cooking, and to my Father, who continues to teach me
what it means to be a 'Real Man'.

Chief Executive Robertsbridge Group   Robert Gunn
Publishing Director   Arthur Severn
Author   Mark MacIntyre
Editor   Margaret Gore
Designer   John Bull
Art Production   The Book Design Company
Assistant Editor   Chuck Smeeton
Production Manager   Greg Howell
Talent Co-ordinator   Laini Gunn
Typesetting   The Typographers
Photography   Karl Schwerdtfeger Jon Love
Food Stylists   Robert Carmak Belinda Frank Yvonne Hicks
Printing   Hannan Print
Marketing Services   Harrison KLP
Project Co-ordinator   Moe Wiseman

Publisher
Robertsbridge Severn
Member of the Robertsbridge Group of Los Angeles
New York, London and Sydney

LA Office
Suite 1951
1888 Century Park East
Los Angeles CA 90067

International Distributors

T.B. Clarke (Overseas) Pty Ltd
302 Bronte Road
Waverley, NSW 2024
Telephone (02) 389 8488 Fax (02) 387 7623

T.B. Clarke (UK) Distributors Ltd
Beckett House
14 Billings Road
Northampton, UK NN1 5AW
Telephone (0604) 23 0941 Fax (0604) 23 0942

T.B. Clarke (USA) Inc.
150 North Autumn Street
San Jose, CA 95110 USA
Telephone (408) 298 3322 Fax (408) 286 3077

Published in association with Century Publishing

MacIntyre, Mark, 1956–
Real man's cookbook
ISBN 0 947178 64 3
1. Cookery I. Title
641.5

CONTENTS

Mark MacIntyre's
Cooking Philosophy

When approached to write this book, I blanched (pun most definitely intended).

I like to cook. Always have, probably always will. But in no way, shape or form do I profess to be a *cordon* anything' chef, nor do I aspire to work in a four-star hotel or restaurant. I simply enjoy creating tasty, nutritious and well-presented meals that take a minimum of physical and psychic trauma to prepare. My personal favourite cooking environment is the 'barbecue', for three important reasons:

1. Food always tastes better outdoors, regardless of what you make.

2. Outdoor sports and activities are splendidly distracting devices when the food is less than perfect. Burn your burgers? No problem. Organise a spur-of-the-moment cricket or football match.

3. Food always tastes better outdoors, regardless of what you make.

Cooking is also an escape for me. One that, on balance, is apparently much less destructive than substance abuse. Not necessarily less expensive, but certainly less destructive. My job and lifestyle have evolved into what one might refer to as a classic example of the 'five kilos of beans in a two-kilo bag' syndrome. In another apparently unwritten law of nature, my personal and professional activities expand in both quantity and duration to fill all available time.

As a result, I use cooking as a method to 're-connect' planetarily and take a breather from the day's whirlwind of events, deadlines and schedules. When I'm in the kitchen, all bets are off. I am totally in control. Turn on the telephone answering machine, put on some Al Green or Miles Davis's 'Kind of Blue', and unwind. Improvise a lot, following an instinct or an ''I wonder what would happen if …'' scenario.

The style and format of this book may also be seen as a reaction to what I feel is an alarming trend toward 'Cookbook as Artbook'. When perusing the shelves of your local bookseller, notice how many cookbooks are oversized, overpriced and seem destined for the coffee table rather than the kitchen table. This is a working cookbook! It is designed specifically to get spattered, dropped, immersed and unintentionally greased. I invite you to get familiar with 'The Real Man's Cookbook'. Agree with it, amend it, embellish on it, but, above all, use it as a launching pad, not a destination. Cooking should be fun, not a chore. The rest is up to you. Go for it!

INTRODUCTION
WHY REAL MEN COOK

Through exhaustive research, it has been determined that we 'Real Men' cook for six major reasons:

1. Food will not cook itself.
2. Cooking ensures our food is dead.
3. We cannot locate or convince someone else (usually of the opposite sex) to cook for us.
4. We like to cook.
5. We think we like to cook.
6. Other real men tell us we like to cook (see 5).

Some of us see cooking as a fun, creative, thought-provoking process, one which demands a certain amount of systems-analysis ability, decision-making skills and the capacity to think critically. Others would prefer to have oral surgery performed on them.

Should you discover you are particularly well suited to cooking and actually enjoy it, plunge in by all means! I would also encourage you to supplement your cooking library with additional volumes since this book is written for the other 97 per cent of the readers who view cooking as an unsavoury, unavoidable life task, similar to walking the dog, taking out the trash, cutting the lawn and watching subtitled foreign films.

When time and circumstance allow, by all means stretch your creative wings. You will find the kitchen to be a unique physical and psychic environment where you are in total control. *You* control the combination and preparation of ingredients, *you* control the heat level and duration, and *you* control the ultimate presentation of the dish.

Remember: When it comes to cooking – innovate, don't replicate!

Experimentation is the only reason we're not still squatting around a fire, greasy up to our elbows, belching and grunting (although that sounds similar to several camping trips I've been on!). Good cooking, like good sex, should be a fun, creative and mutually rewarding activity, accomplished with a dash of flair and lots of positive energy.

As for more than one person in the kitchen at a time, I think it's fine as long as one person is kibitzing, making small talk and perhaps having a glass of wine, while the other person prepares the food and cooks, *alone!* Having two chefs in the kitchen is like having two ranking generals on the battlefield, two skippers at the helm of a boat, or a team of two driving a car... an invitation to disaster!

In addition to the aforementioned reasons for cooking, it can be further categorised into two predominant modes:

I. Survival.
II. Strategic.

In 'Survival' mode cooking, most activity takes place late at night or early in the morning and usually reflects the amount of time available for performing a given number of tasks (see also: 'Five Kilos of Beans in a Two-Kilo Bag'). This culinary style is often guided by a frame of mind induced by having just spent more hours at the office in a single day than you've spent on the tennis court all season.

The term *cooking* applies only in the strictest technical sense here, since this mode is characterised by placing food and foodstuffs in one's mouth as rapidly as possible, with little or no consideration to preparation and presentation. 'Survival' cooking normally takes place in a dark kitchen, illuminated only by the fridge light and can be recognised by the dishevelled 'cook' assuming a half-crouching position in front of the open fridge door and performing a distinctive wrist-to-chin, shovelling, arm motion.

Under these circumstances all manner of edibles and quasi-edibles become fair game. Only those most closely resembling a school science project are passed over. Indeed, dishes prepared in 'Survival' mode cooking generally require little or no heating. This is a function of the extraordinarily narrow 'window of opportunity' between container occupancy and gnashing molars.

The end of a 'Survival' cooking meal is signalled by the absence of additional edible material and/or cataclysmic gastric disturbance. In either case, the rumpled cook/diner often repairs to a position directly in front of a television set where he watches late sports results, a recap of the day's global disasters or tomorrow's weather. He promptly falls asleep there, fully or partially clothed, illuminated only by the stroboscopic flicker of the telly, only to awaken to test patterns a few hours later. He then shuffles off to bed to catch a few hours of sleep before embarking on a 'bright new day'.

'Strategic' cooking, on the other hand, is that behaviour which attempts to communicate (usually with a desirable member of the opposite sex) the notion that you are no stranger to kitchen appliances other than the can opener. It is your brilliant stab at convincing friends, family and prospective partners that you are truly a hip, sensitive, macho, aware, contemporary kind of guy, a 'Real Man's' real man.

Although intensive, first-hand research has unequivocally shown that a majority of women are undeniably attracted to men who are at least marginally adroit in the kitchen, a word of caution is necessary. It's important not to appear too skilled in the kitchen! Like other personal and professional skills, the ability to prepare delicious meals efficiently and effectively is governed by the law of diminishing returns. Appear 'too good to be true' in the kitchen and women generally respond in two ways:

1. They're irretrievably intimidated and shut you down cold, or
2. They're overwhelmed with joy and suddenly forever forget which end of a pot to hold!

Either way, you lose. Not unlike professional life, in 'strategic' cooking it's important that you not do a job 'too well', as that only makes people directly above and below you very uncomfortable.

Remember: You're trying to communicate that you are the most mature, sensitive, masterful and 'together' guy this woman has ever seen, not that you're a Cordon Bleu chef who's not happy unless you have a wooden spoon in your hand!

WHAT 'REAL MEN' NEED TO COOK

The necessities of good cooking can be broken into two main subgroups: 'Hardware' and 'Software'. The former covers stove, pots, pans, racks and utensils, while the latter includes main ingredients, herbs and spices. Before purchasing items from either category, spend a little time doing research at markets, butcher shops, fishmongers, restaurant supply houses and better department stores. Get to know what 'the best' means, in trade terms, and how to recognise it *before* you buy. An educated consumer is a wise shopper and most frequently satisfied.

HARDWARE

The Stove

The primary heat source, usually fired by gas, electricity, wood or coal. Gas is the most desirable, from a temperature-control standpoint, followed closely by electricity, with everything else tied for last place. Microwave ovens, which use microwave radiation to thaw, warm and cook food, fit into this category, but only loosely. They should be used solely for what they

do best – that is, heating up leftovers. Anything more technically demanding usually produces dismal results. Never send a plumber to do an electrician's job. Cook in the oven or on the stove top, reheat in a microwave.

Pots and Pans

If you look at cooking as a textural, consumable art, your pots and pans are the palette on which your organic 'colours' are blended. Your best bet is to purchase a boxed starter set (approximately 12–15 pieces) to begin with, as it is usually far cheaper than buying 'open stock' or separate pieces. In terms of materials and construction, look for a bottom of copper (the most efficient, even-heat conductant) with sides and interior walls of high-quality stainless steel.

Look for good, sturdy handles, with the most desirable being ovenproof. Solid aluminium, while suitable for aeronautical materials and some primitive camp cookware, has little application in the 'Real Man's' kitchen. It distributes heat dismally, is tough to clean and occasionally reacts to some acidic foods. Cast iron, while romantically linked to the pioneer days, is an absolute nightmare to clean. Regardless, your array of cookware needs to include at least one huge black 'Dutch Oven' or stewpot. Keep a scouring pad handy!

Recently, many folks have been taking a hard look at several brands of tempered-glass, stovetop cookware, which is convenient due to its micro-wave-safe capacity. My advice: Avoid it like the plague! It's horrific at heat distribution and dissipation (your food continues to cook long after you've cut the heat). Save ovenproof glass for casseroles, baking dishes and the like. Likewise, steer clear of pans coated with 'space-age by-products' that prevent food from sticking. These plastic-like surfaces scratch easily and the jury's still out on the effects of long-term exposure to their fumes as they heat. Stick with potentially sticky surfaces but just keep a closer eye on your cooking and don't let pots and pans sit for several days before washing up. You'll do just fine!

Utensils

Core components to your utensil armoury should be a good set of cutlery and a slotted hardwood block in which to keep them. Used properly and sharpened regularly, a set of knives will last you a lifetime, so don't hesitate to spend a little extra to get the best (again, like in pots and pans, buying a complete starter set will probably be cheaper than buying each knife individually). High carbon stainless steel is the *only* choice in blade material, and handles should be wood or synthetic, riveted for durability and shaped for hand comfort. If necessary, ask your butcher for advice on how to sharpen knives properly.

Other important kitchen components include a sturdy spatula, a two-tined fork, a large slotted spoon, a medium-sized whisk, a measuring cup, a nest of measuring spoons, a nest of mixing bowls (in graduated sizes), a medium-sized sieve, colander and a large wooden spoon or two.

Other helpful devices include a meat thermometer, garlic press (although I prefer to buy my garlic pre-minced in 125 g bottles), a juicer, a blender, a food processor and several fire-resistant potholders. For other detailed information, consult your mother!

Dishware/Flatware/Glassware

Keep it simple! Outfit your table with the following guidance in mind:

1. Dishware (two sets) should be white, since colours distract you from what's on your plate. One set porcelain and one set unbreakable.
2. Flatware should be simply designed, high-quality stainless steel, with as little rococo scrollwork and filigree as possible.
3. Glassware should be clear, easy to hold and should not be decorated with corporate logotypes, cartoon characters, tourist attractions or hunting and fishing scenes.

SOFTWARE

Predominant in this category are the ingredients you cook with. ALWAYS BUY THE BEST, THE FRESHEST AVAILABLE! You can't end up with a stunning meal if you start with average ingredients. Spend time getting to know what exactly 'the best' means in terms of fruit, vegetables, meat, fish and poultry. Talk to butchers, bakers and greengrocers, and other folks who care about preparing food properly. Ask for their favourite 'trade secrets' to identify the best, freshest ingredients. Learn to sniff, poke, scratch, thump and look at everything you buy with a hypercritical eye.

To get familiar with herbs, here's a handy tip someone gave me: Get about ½ kg of freshly ground mince and shape it into as many ping pong ball-sized meatballs as you can. Purchase (or borrow) tins of sage, basil, rosemary, thyme, dill, marjoram, cumin and whatever else strikes your fancy. Add a pinch of spice to each meatball (one spice per meatball) and cook to your taste. Enjoy the meatballs individually, unadorned except for their respective herb seasoning. This will acquaint you with the flavour of each herb for later reference. Try this a couple of times to 'lock in' the flavour and taste.

If you're preparing a special or 'strategic' meal, by all means visit speciality or gourmet shops. Although supermarkets are convenient and sell items of utilitarian quality, there's simply no way to beat the knowledge, reputation for quality and human contact with a greengrocer, fishmonger or butcher. They can be invaluably helpful in offering cooking suggestions, appropriate quantities and high quality in foodstuffs.

COOKING TIPS, TRICKS AND TRADE SECRETS FOR THE 'REAL MAN'

Cooking, like most other realms of human behaviour, is invisibly governed by certain absolute laws of physical nature. Being well acquainted with these 'rules of thumb' will save endless hours of frustration, anger and violence. You will probably discover some of your own along the way which you may add to this list:

1. The probability that you'll irretrievably ruin a particularly pricey cut of meat, fish or poultry increases exponentially in direct proportion to:
    (a) The number of dollars in purchase price.
    (b) The number of hours you've invested in preparation.
    (c) The relative importance of the occasion.
    (d) The lack of time available to prepare a suitable, alternative dish.

2. The chances that the spice jar you reach for will be empty increase exponentially in direct proportion to the relative importance of that particular spice to the recipe you're preparing.

3. If you apply any spreadable substance to any manner of bread, roll, muffin or biscuit and that same item promptly slips from your grasp, it will inevitably land 'butter-side-down'.

4. Regardless of how carefully you slice a bagel or hardroll in preparation for toasting, and irrespective of the size of the slots in your toaster, only one slice will fit. The other will require substantial stuffing, poking and jamming and will inevitably self-immolate.

5. Regardless of the application, you will inevitably prepare more rice than you need.

6. If you prepare a recipe requiring the use of tinned tomato paste, regardless of the nature or size of the recipe, you will always be left with half a tin of tomato paste.

7. Here is a glossary/equivalents chart for some frequently used cooking terms:
    1 'smidge' = ½ 'skosh'
    1 'skosh' = 2.5 'pinches'

1 'pinch' = 3–4 'sprinkles'
1 large 'splash' = 2 'dashes'
1 'drip' = 1 'drizzle' + ½ large 'splash'
1 'sizeable wad' = ½ 'whole bunch'
1 'whole bunch' = ¼ 'massive gob'

RECIPES

The following recipes are divided, by no particular flash of divine inspiration, into Breakfast, Informal Entertaining, Special Occasions and Family Barbecues. Each of these has its own social requirements and I try to reflect the mood accordingly.

Someone once told me that the most important cooking utensil God gave us was our hands and that they should be used extensively in preparation for adding ingredients, mixing and tasting. This makes a lot of sense, not only from an efficiency and convenience standpoint, but it also allows us to get physically close to the food we're preparing. So before you start, roll up your sleeves, get the water good and hot and scrub as though you were preparing for surgery. And have some fun!

BREAKFASTS

Eggs Benedict

4 crumpets or muffins

4 slices of ham

4 eggs

butter

Hollandaise sauce
3 egg yolks

50 g butter

1 tablespoon wine vinegar

salt and pepper to taste

Another apocryphal dish. Almost everyone recognises the name, but only 10 per cent of the human population has actually ever had it. You seldom get it at home, which reminds me of a particularly racy eggs benedict joke which has no place in a family cookbook (send me your name, address and a self-addressed stamped envelope, together with proof you're over 18, care of my publisher, and I'll mail you the joke). Eggs benedict is not an everyday dish, but for special, even 'strategic' occasions, it's tough to beat. Try it, it's not as hard as you think. The sheep are separated from the goats in hollandaise sauce making!

To make the hollandaise sauce, first melt the butter in a double saucepan over hot water. Add the egg yolks and vinegar to the melted butter and stir smartly until the sauce is smooth and thick. Then add salt and pepper to taste. The secret of 'mega' hollandaise: NEVER let it boil!

Toast and butter the crumpets or muffins and set aside in a warm place, away from gaping mouths and gnashing molars. Poach the eggs. Lay a slice of ham on each crumpet/muffin. Place a poached egg on top of each piece of ham.

Finally, cover the eggs with the hollandaise sauce and serve immediately with a garnish of parsley. Serves 4 (it's a really good joke!).

MUESLI

Makes approximately 700 g

175 g rolled oats

125 g cornflakes

100 g wheatgerm

100 g bran

25 g sultanas

75 g finely chopped dried apricot

75 g finely chopped dried apple

25 g sunflower seeds

50 g unsalted chopped mixed nuts

50 g desiccated coconut

unrefined brown sugar to taste

If I had to pick my favourite breakfast dish, I'd have to say 'cereal'. Okay, okay! I know it's boring, but I like it! I'm in this for the long haul so I'm all for bulking up my diet with extra fibre. And cereal is one of the best sources. It's also easy to digest, doesn't take a lot of preparation and you feel good after eating it! Here's a winning muesli combination with a multitude of fruit and grain components...

Simply combine the ingredients well (that wasn't hard, was it?) in a locking plastic bag or plastic container with an airtight lid. Note: There are as many muesli blends as there are grains, fruits and blenders. Add what you like! Eat with low-fat milk, yoghurt and top with fresh fruit. You'll love it!

Oatmeal Muffins

250 g self-raising flour

175 g quick-cooking rolled oats

zest of 1 lemon

2 eggs, beaten

250 mL orange juice

3 tablespoons vegetable oil

Preheat the oven to 200°C.

Okay! Okay! I confess! I'm a big muffin man. Always have been, always will be. Good *home-made* muffins (the store-bought versions are usually suited only for tossing at noisy pets and unruly children) are the perfect energy- and nutrition-packed breakfast food for those of us who arise and are automatically three hours behind schedule. Recently my days have been beginning so early I feel like a Buddhist monk! What do I have as I 'bottoms-up' my cuppa and head for the door? A muffin, about as big as a small melon, sliced, with a swipe of margarine and marmalade.

Sift the flour into a baking bowl. Sifted flour is important! Don't let anyone tell you otherwise. Add the oats and lemon zest and mix well. Make a well in the centre of the flour and pour in the beaten eggs, orange juice and vegetable oil. Stir only six turns, or until just combined. (Do not overstir muffin batter. It should yield lumpy, bumpy muffins, not those computer-generated disasters we see in supermarkets!)

Grease your muffin tray (you do *have* a muffin tray, don't you!?). Fill the tray approximately two-thirds the way up each muffin mould. Bake in the oven until bumpy, golden and delicious looking, approximately 20 minutes. Serves 6 (non-muffin mavens).

'SPECIAL EDITION' FRENCH TOAST

8 slices fruit bread

3 eggs

125 mL whole milk

125 mL single cream

80 g sugar

few drops of vanilla essence

1 teaspoon ground
  cinnamon

pinch nutmeg

2 tablespoons unsalted
  butter

30 g icing sugar

Here's the perfect breakfast for a lazy, low-key Sunday – one of those days when the most constructive thing you do all day is read the paper! Especially appropriate after active indoor sports! This recipe takes French Toast several steps further to its natural culinary conclusion. The secret ingredients – vanilla essence and nutmeg.

Try this as part of a 'strategic' meal sequence. If it doesn't work or only produces marginal results, re-think your strategy, join a health club, or begin attending church religiously. On second thoughts, begin attending church anyway!

Place the eggs in bowl (removing their shells first!) and add the milk and cream. Take the mixture and beat it like a crazy person. Add the sugar, cinnamon, vanilla essence and nutmeg. Beat again until the sugar dissolves. Pour into a large flat baking dish.

Heat the butter in a heavy-based frying pan over medium heat. Dip the bread slices into the egg mixture so that they soak it up, but not to the point where they start to crumble. When they crumble, the party's over.

Fry the bread slices, a few at a time, on each side until they are golden brown. Remove and drain on absorbent kitchen paper. Place on a warm serving dish and dust with sifted icing sugar. Shoot the calorie 'wad' and serve with conserve, marmalade or honey. Rates about 9 million calories, enough to keep a small village in Antarctica warm for about a week. Or serves 4 adults!

Mushroom and Sweetcorn Ramekins

125 g button mushrooms

220 g sweetcorn kernels

1 tablespoon unsalted butter

6 tablespoons low-fat
  yoghurt

6 eggs

pinch of nutmeg

2 tablespoons chopped
  chives

60 g grated gruyere cheese

salt and freshly ground
  black pepper to taste

When I need to roll out the 'heavy artillery' for a power breakfast, mushroom and sweetcorn ramekins are tops on the list. The vegetable ingredients provide an interesting counterpoint to the egg and yoghurt and they're bloody good for you too! Try this one when you're tired of eggs benedict, poached baby trout and lark's tongue in aspic. I'm sure you'll be pleasantly surprised. Especially good on autumn or winter mornings.

Deal with the mushrooms first. Wipe them with a clean, damp cloth (NEVER wash or peel!) and slice thinly. Melt the butter in a saucepan and gently sauté.

Preheat the oven to 180°C.

Take six ramekin dishes (or as many as you've got!) and place a tablespoon of yoghurt in each. Carefully count each kernel of corn … only kidding! … and divide evenly between the ramekins. Crack an egg into each and top with the sautéed mushrooms. Season to taste with salt and pepper. Sprinkle with the nutmeg and chopped chives. Finally, top with grated cheese.

Deftly stand the ramekins in a baking dish that's filled with enough hot water to reach half-way up the sides (of the ramekins). Bake in the oven for 15–20 minutes. Serve with hot buttered toast. Serves 6 (single ramekin people).

Classic French Omelette A La The Kitchen Sink

For each omelette:

3 eggs

1 tablespoon water

¼ teaspoon salt

1 tablespoon butter

ground white pepper
 to taste

This recipe got its name when someone asked me what I put in it. "Everything but the kitchen sink," I replied. And the name stuck. Basically you can put virtually anything organic (and tasty!) inside. Experiment! Try to steer clear of really juicy things as they tend to make omelettes runny. And there's nothing worse than runny omelettes! Well, maybe a few things…

Beat the eggs, water, salt and pepper together in a bowl while heating a heavy skillet over a medium-high heat. Add the butter. When the foam subsides, add the egg mixture. Cook the eggs until they are just set on the bottom and then, with an appropriate utensil (spatula), gently push the cooked portion of the omelette into the centre of the pan, allowing the uncooked mixture to flow underneath onto the cooking surface.

The 'kitchen sink' filling is exactly that: Everything you can rustle up from the fridge. As long as it looks non-toxic, toss it in. Grated cheese, mushrooms, chopped herbs, seeded and diced red or green capsicum, shredded ham, skinned and chopped tomato, chopped spring onions, cooked zucchini, onion, cooked bacon, bits of sausage – you name it! Everything is 'fair game'!

Spoon the 'kitchen sink' mixture onto one half of the omelette and fold the other half on top. Gently slide the omelette onto a plate and serve with hot buttered toast. Serves 1 (person per omelette).

DROP SCONES

125 g self-raising flour

¼ teaspoon bicarbonate
of soda

pinch of salt

30 g sugar

1 egg, beaten

150 mL milk, soured with
1 teaspoon lemon juice

1 tablespoon butter, melted

Not to be confused with a 'drop kick' or 'drop zone', this particular recipe gets its name from the physical action required to make these most delectable of scones. I became a scones convert upon my first trip to England, where I consumed them at a startling rate, gaining nearly two stone in the process. Note: If you don't use self-raising flour, don't expect scones. Some small glutinous masses that are dark on one side, perhaps suitable for dropping medium-sized birds on the wing, but not scones. Get some real, thick-cut marmalade (you know, the type with golfball-sized chunks of rind) and slather it on. Heaven!

Sift the flour and bicarbonate of soda, salt and sugar into a baking bowl. Make a well in the centre and add the beaten egg, milk and melted butter. Stir well, then beat to form a smooth, thick batter.

Heat a greased griddle or large heavy-based frying pan over medium heat. Drop spoonfuls of the batter onto the pan and cook until bubbles begin to burst on the surface of the scones. Flip them over (here's the fun part) and cook until they are risen, cooked through and light brown on both sides. Remove and keep in a warm place (other than next to your heart, you sentimental fool!). Repeat until all the batter is used. Serve with whipped butter, jam, marmalade or maple syrup. Serves 8 (serves 2 if you don't use the self-raising flour!).

BARBECUES

2 bottles good red wine

2–3 kilograms of ribs
(beef or pork)*

1 large onion, chopped

1 large green capsicum,
chopped

1 large red capsicum,
chopped

2–3 cloves garlic, peeled
and crushed

340 g can crushed, peeled
tomatoes

75 g can tomato paste

1 teaspoon salt

2 teaspoons black pepper

1 tablespoon tabasco sauce
or to taste

70 mL Tequila

½ can beer

1 tablespoon butter
or margarine

2 teaspoons soy sauce

2 teaspoons chilli powder

juice of one lemon

2 tablespoons extra virgin
olive oil

1 tablespoon molasses

⅓ cup fine brown sugar

*Depends on the
size/number of
dinner guests.

RIBS AROUND THE WORLD

Rib Philosophy

Please feel free to share these recipes with friends; they're a lot like money – it doesn't work unless you spread it around.

Firstly, you must start with fresh ribs, beef or pork. If they're frozen you may as well call for take-away Chinese instead. An age-old debate continues to rage as to which is more aesthetically correct: beef or pork ribs. I like 'em both. Switch around and give 'em both a try. Also, experiment with recipes – that's how I got to be 'Rib King' three years running.

Secondly, when in doubt, MARINATE, MARINATE, MARINATE. The actual key to my rib success lies in my marinating the little beauties for days (at least 24 hours). Marinating makes up for a lot in terms of tenderness and flavour. I've seen very borderline ribs become works of culinary art after sufficient marinating. The Tequila does something to the muscle fibre (my doctor friend says it denatures the proteins or something like that).

Thirdly, use top-quality herbs and spices in your marinade and don't even think about using that wizened old clump of garlic off the shelf. You know, the one that upon inspection resembles a first-prize winner at a science fair. For crying out loud, splash out and buy a fresh specimen!

As for quantity – that's a very sticky wicket, indeed! After all there are rib eaters and there are RIB EATERS. Suggesting weights like a half-kilogram per person is tough because so much is non-edible. Start with a kilogram per person if they are not big eaters but revise upwards dramatically if you're dealing with a football team or people recently rescued from a desert island. The nice thing about ribs is they keep wonderfully in the refrigerator and, like meatloaf and certain Italian dishes, actually taste better the more they're reheated.

Ribs continued

And a Word about Cooking Appliances

Traditionally, ribs are prepared on a barbecue that features a mesh or grate-like cooking surface. That way the excess fat (of which there is often a considerable amount) drips through the grate and actually adds to the 'integrity' of the heat source (propane gas, lava rocks, natural wood, coals, etc.). The grating separates the cooks from the sauciers as well, since the fire will soon be totally out of control if the ribs aren't dutifully manipulated and watched. Cooking on a flat, metallic hot plate is somewhat less desirable, since you might as well prepare them at home in the frying pan!

The Marinade Sauce

Using the largest, deepest frying pan you can lay your hands on, heat the olive oil over medium heat. Add the garlic, onions, capsicum, pinch of salt and pepper. Sauté until the onions are translucent. Add the beer and Tequila, being careful not to ignite the latter. Stir gently. Add the crushed tomatoes and tomato paste, keeping the heat even. Sprinkle in the chilli powder. Reduce heat slightly and add the lemon juice, molasses and brown sugar which should be completely dissolved. Cook covered for 20 minutes. Add the remaining ingredients individually, using tabasco, salt and pepper to taste. Melt in the butter or margarine. Cook over a low heat for an extra 10 minutes or so, or until your neighbours begin appearing to investigate the smell.

Open the first bottle of red wine and allow it to breathe for 15 minutes or so.

I love my ribs spicy so I have a heavy hand with the tabasco. Be careful because a little too much and your ribs will be inedibly hot.

Now reduce heat and let your marinade cool. Pour a glass of red wine and sip it slowly.

Ribs continued

Now reduce heat and let your marinade cool. Pour a glass of red wine and sip it slowly.

The ribs should be prepared by rinsing them carefully and dropping them into furiously boiling water for three minutes. Remove them immediately and allow to cool. When both the ribs and marinade are cool, rub ribs with the pulp of the lemon squeezed for the marinade and lay them out in a single layer in the bottom of a large plastic or earthenware tray. The bigger your ribs, the bigger the tray(s). Tupperware™ is excellent in this instance. The snap-on lid keeps the marinade fragrance from infiltrating everything else in your refrigerator. Cover the ribs completely with marinade. Refrigerate for at least 6 to 12 hours (preferably 24 hours). The idea here is to allow the meat to really absorb the flavour of the Tequila and other goodies.

Retire with the rest of the red wine and a good book.

Cooking

Open the second bottle of red wine and allow it to breathe.

Keep your ribs in their covered container for travelling. Be careful not to spill any sauce on your clothing as there's no known solvent. When you arrive at your picnic (or backyard) barbecue, fire up the grill and build a nice bed of coals (if it's a propane grill, just get it really hot). Pour yourself a glass of red wine and sip slowly. Remove the ribs (which have been cut into two or three ribs per piece) and place on the grill. Keep your eye on them as they cook and rotate frequently. Refill your glass with red wine.

If the dripping fat and resulting inferno becomes unmanageable in one area, keep the meat shifting, not allowing too much fat to soak through in one area. The leaner the ribs, the less you'll have to worry about fat fire flare-ups. Cook for

Ribs continued

7 to 10 minutes on each side or until carbon begins to appear. Don't overcook, but don't indulge in pork sushi either.

Pour yourself some more red or crack open some beer, roll up your sleeves and dig in. Remember: bones store the heat for a long time so be careful when grasping your greasy morsels. Always use mugs for drinks since all other glass vessels have a habit of squirting through greasy hands! Serve with corn bread and okra or mixed greens.

MARK'S RUMP ROAST

1.5 kg rump roast

2 tablespoons olive oil

2 cloves garlic, peeled and crushed

1 teaspoon Dijon mustard

1 teaspoon soy sauce

½ teaspoon rosemary

2 tablespoons white wine vinegar

60 mL sweet white wine

2 tablespoons tomato sauce

1 teaspoon Worcestershire sauce

Okay, all you wise guys out there, this recipe has nothing to do with roasting my rump, although the concept *does* bring to mind a couple of upper-management meetings I've attended recently! Like most barbecue cookery applications, marinating is the key step in the process. I frequently double, sometimes triple, the suggested marinating times, using the marinade as a saviour for average cuts of meat.

If you're lucky enough to be barbecuing outside, where God himself intended (none of these indoor, electric, ultrasonic microwave-enhanced contraptions for me!), be sure to make your cooking environment as non-hostile as possible. Non-hostile accoutrements include:

(1) a floppy hat and sun block if it's sunny;
(2) an umbrella and rainwear if the weather forecast calls for 'partly sunny' or 'mostly cloudy';
(3) a small transistor radio to listen to music or sport;
(4) a newspaper of some description;
(5) a folding lawn chair; and
(6) one or more bottles of beer.

Place the oil in a heavy-based frying pan and sauté the garlic for 2 minutes. Remove the pan from the heat and stir in the mustard, soy sauce, rosemary, vinegar and wine.

Place the roast in a large baking dish and pour the sauce over the meat. Turn the meat so it's well coated with sauce. Cover the dish tightly with plastic wrap and pop in the fridge for at least 24 hours, periodically turning the meat in the marinade.

Preheat the barbecue. Drain the meat and reserve the marinade. Add the tomato and Worcestershire sauces to the marinade and stir well. Using a pastry brush (avoid using anything turned up from years in the tool shed, dripping with multicolour, viscous substances), coat the meat well with the marinade.

At this stage, and depending on the relative fire-resistance of your guests' mouths, you might well want to introduce a little tabasco sauce here as well.

Carefully cook roast on the barbecue, turning frequently, for approximately 40–45 minutes, or until it's cooked to your taste. Serves 6.

LAMB LEG CHOPS

8 thick lamb leg chops

175 mL olive oil

juice of 1 lemon

1 onion, peeled and
  chopped

1 teaspoon oregano

salt and black pepper to taste

Garnish
lemon slices

onion slices

parsley sprigs

After years of languishing in outdoor obscurity, lamb is finally taking its rightful place in the barbecue popularity hall of fame. Since it's a delicate, rather lean meat, before you light up your barbecue, wipe the grill with absorbent kitchen paper sprinkled with vegetable oil. Then rub a little into the lamb chops just before you pop them on. This prevents them from sticking as they cook.

Lamb and garlic seem to have been created for each other. Go ahead and give a free hand to the garlic demons in your head. Decide on breath-neutralising strategies later!

In a bowl, combine the olive oil, lemon juice, chopped onions and oregano. Season to taste with salt and pepper. Place the chops in a baking dish and pour the marinade over them. Cover the dish (to prevent marinade-flavoured trifle in your fridge) and place in the fridge for at least 3–4 hours.

Drain the chops and reserve the marinade for basting. Cook the chops on the preheated barbecue, brushing them copiously with marinade, for about 5 minutes a side or to your taste (NO LAMB SUSHI!). Serve garnished with lemon and onion slices, sprinkled with fresh parsley. Serves 4.

BUTTERFLY LEG OF LAMB

2.5 kg leg of lamb, boned
(have the butcher bone it,
leaving the seam open)

250 mL good red wine

200 mL good chicken stock

2 tablespoons marmalade

40 mL white wine vinegar

1 small onion, peeled and
finely chopped

2 teaspoons rosemary

1 teaspoon marjoram

1 bay leaf

2 cm fresh root ginger,
peeled and grated

A dish named for the world's most tedious culinary presentation: a short-lived phenomenon that involved barbecuing butterflies' legs. A thankless, time-consuming and inescapably futile task, 'Shank o' Butterfly' required thousands of manhours collecting, sorting and cleaning the human hair-sized limbs, only to have them blow away in a stiff breeze before they even got close to the barbecue. This folly lasted only a few years in the deepest, darkest Middle Ages. It is apparently still offered on a few menus in northern Scotland.

This, like most lamb recipes utilising the barbecue, is simply delectable. For best results, use 'Industrial Strength' thick-cut marmalade only.

In a heavy-based saucepan, combine the wine, chicken stock, marmalade, vinegar, onion, herbs and ginger. Season to taste with salt and freshly ground black pepper. Bring to the boil, reduce heat and simmer gently for 15 minutes.

Coax the lamb into a large baking dish and pour marinade over, making sure that the outside is well covered. Cover the dish with plastic wrap and refrigerate for 2 hours.

Preheat the barbecue. Drain the the meat and reserve the marinade for basting. Cook the lamb on the barbecue slowly, turning frequently and basting earnestly with the marinade.

The lamb will take approximately 1 hour to cook. (Note: If you happen to be barbecuing on the surface of the planet Mercury, your skilfully prepared Butterfly Leg of Lamb will be done quite nicely in the time it takes for you to walk from the door of your asbestos house to the backyard 'barbie'. Remember not to step into any steaming fissures and to wear your aviation fire-fighting costume, or you'll be done to a turn as well!) Serves 8 (or 11 Mercurians without stainless steel stomach extensions).

BARBECUED PRAWNS 'GODZILLA'

12 green king prawns

250 mL mirin (sweet, cooking rice wine)

200 mL sake

125 mL dark soy sauce

Garnish
lemon slices

1 small lettuce

2 shallots, finely chopped

Here's a great recipe for those prawns you see in the fishmarket that resemble small saloon cars. It uses Japanese ingredients and the 'less is more' school of cooking psychology.

A delicate rice wine/soy sauce basting liquid is the perfect complement to these 'jewels of the deep'. Experiment by trying oyster sauce in place of soy. I like prawns enough to have them five dinners running! If you feel the same way, try this barbecued method for a change of pace …

Wash the prawns and pat dry with absorbent kitchen paper. If you like you can remove the heads and shell, but there isn't really a need to. Place the prawns onto bamboo skewers. In a small pan, over low to medium heat, combine the mirin, soy sauce and sake. Bring to the boil, reduce heat and simmer until reduced by half. Remove from the heat and brush the prawns with the sauce.

Preheat the barbecue. When hot, cook the prawns for 2–3 minutes per side, copiously basting with the sauce as they cook.

Shred the lettuce and arrange on individual serving plates. Carefully remove the prawns from the skewers and arrange on the beds of lettuce. Garnish with lemon or lime wedges and diced shallots. Serves 4.

ROLLED LEG OF PORK HAWAIIAN STYLE

5.5 kg loin of pork, boned and rolled

1 cup apple sauce

200 mL dry white wine

125 mL soy sauce

2 tablespoons olive oil

1 onion, peeled and finely chopped

1 clove garlic, peeled and crushed

2.5 cm fresh ginger root, peeled and grated

salt and pepper to taste

The 'Grand Kahuna' of pork dishes, served up from the land of white sand beaches, turquoise waters and discount eelskin accessories. Barbecued pork is an institution in America. Many believe it to be the only true 'barbecue'. While beef 'barbecue' *aficionados* will argue that call, I tend to lean toward pork as the ultimate 'software' for outdoor cooking.

This recipe pivots on a garlicky marinade that offers just the right blend of sweet and sour with the snap of ginger root. Do your meat a favour and let it stand several hours in the marinade and always-always-always allow it to warm up to room temperature before placing it on the barbecue. That way it'll cook more evenly and thoroughly.

In a bowl, combine the apple sauce, wine, soy sauce, olive oil, onion, garlic and ginger. Season to taste with salt and freshly ground pepper. Place the rolled pork in a large baking dish and pour marinade over the meat. Marinate in the refrigerator for at least 2 hours, turning the meat from time to time.

Preheat your barbecue. Drain the pork, reserving the marinade, and place the meat on the spit. Roast the pork over medium heat until well done, approximately 3 hours, basting the roast with the marinade. When cooked to your liking (make sure *you're* in charge of quality control!), carefully remove the roast from the spit and set aside to rest for 10–15 minutes before carving. Serves 12 (or 6 and a week's worth of sandwiches).

BARBECUED CHICKEN 'BUSH STYLE'

6 chicken joints, thighs and legs (requires 24-hour marinating)

125 mL cider vinegar

100 mL olive oil

1 teaspoon Worcestershire sauce

2 shallots, finely chopped

1 clove garlic, peeled and chopped

1 teaspoon paprika

2 teaspoons tomato purée

6 dashes tabasco sauce

½ teaspoon German mustard

30 g butter, melted

salt and pepper to taste

If you've ever had the opportunity to eat in the bush, any bush, I'm sure you'll agree that it's one of those activities – like wilderness winter camping – that looks a lot better 'on paper' than it is in actual experience. It's dirty, either blistering hot or bone-chilling cold and there are lots of critters that are dead determined to either share your food or chow down on you! Now, don't get me wrong. I like hiking, camping and fishing probably more than the next person, but I'm sorry! Multi-course meals prepared up to 1 km away from the nearest running water or electrical outlet are, as my grandfather used to say, 'disasters waiting to happen'. Let's be frank, most people's idea of wilderness cuisine is fishing rods and a can of Spam.

Here's an excellent way to savour the vigour and vitality of the 'great outdoors' while lounging in your own backyard, but a few short steps from flush toilets, refrigeration and Sunday newspapers! Viva la Civilisation!

In a bowl (imagining you're 20 kilometres from the nearest coin-box phone), combine the vinegar, oil, Worcestershire sauce, shallots, garlic, paprika, tomato purée, tabasco sauce and mustard. Season to taste with salt and freshly ground pepper (pretending to swat away bothersome flies and wasps).

Then (flicking imaginary debris from them) place the chicken joints in a large flat baking dish and pour the marinade over. Cover with plastic wrap (largely unavailable in remote alpine regions or arid savannah) and refrigerate for at least 24 hours.

Drain the chicken and reserve the marinade. Allow the joints to come up to room temperature for approximately 10–15 minutes. Preheat your barbecue to 'hot' (or 'inferno') setting. Brush the chicken with the melted butter and cook to your liking, brushing with the marinade as you turn the joints. Serves 6.

BINGHAMTON CHICKEN WINGS

800 g chicken wings

125 mL soy sauce

'shot' of tequila

2 tablespoons olive oil

zest and juice of 1 orange

20 mL concentrated orange juice

1 tablespoon Hoi Sin sauce

1 tablespoon honey

2 cm fresh ginger root, peeled and grated

1 clove garlic, crushed

1 tablespoon tabasco sauce

salt and pepper to taste

In America, Buffalo, New York, has become nationally synonymous with spicy, garlicky, barbecued chicken wings. But here's a barbecued wing recipe for another extra-ordinarily average upstate New York town that blows their Buffalo brethren away! Binghamton boasts a Dante's Inferno-esque Greyhound Bus terminal that I've found myself in, for various reasons, many more times than I like to remember. So here's to Binghamton, the women of the State University of New York, and the Greyhound terminal. Long may you wave! These wings are great as starters *or* a main course. (Note: you'll need 10–15 per person for a main course. Have plenty of absorbent kitchen paper and finger bowls available!)

In a bowl, combine the soy sauce, tequila, oil, zest and juice of the orange, orange juice, Hoi Sin sauce, tabasco, honey, ginger and garlic. Season to taste with salt and pepper.

Place the chicken wings in a large baking dish and pour the marinade over. Cover the dish with plastic wrap and refrigerate for at least 4–6 hours (overnight is better!).

Drain the chicken wings and reserve the marinade. Preheat the barbecue. Cook the wings, turning frequently and brushing with the marinade for 7–8 minutes or until cooked through and tender. Note: Keep an eagle eye on them as they cook. With the tequila, sugar (from the honey) and fat combined, they'll want to self-immolate. Be vigilant with the barbecue fork. Serve with barbecue beans, a mixed green salad and an ample supply of cold beer. Serves 6.

SPICY BEEF KEBABS

1 kg sirloin steak

5 cm fresh ginger root, peeled and sliced

2 cloves garlic, peeled and crushed

1 onion, peeled and chopped

250 mL soy sauce

1 tablespoon sugar

8 small dried red chilli peppers, seeded and finely chopped

2 tablespoons cider vinegar

30 g cornflour

125 mL water

When making beef kebabs, always start with *outstanding* beef. Nothing's worse than watching your guests tongue-wrestle with the remains of a steer that was apparently walked to death. Especially if this is a 'strategic' occasion and you're trying desperately to impress the other party. For this dish, start with top sirloin. You can't miss! Watch out for those chillies, they'll rock your planets!

Using a sharp knife, cut the steak into bite-sized cubes. Combine the ginger, garlic, onion, soy sauce, sugar, chilli peppers and vinegar in a small saucepan.

(Note: After cutting or dicing particularly hot chillies, be sure to wash your hands right away. This will prevent you from absent-mindedly rubbing or wiping your eyes with potentially harmful juices and oils.)

Place over medium heat, bring to the boil, reduce heat and simmer for approximately 2 minutes or until the mixture thickens slightly. Blend the cornflour with the water and mix until smooth. Remove saucepan from the heat and stir in the cornflour liquid. Return to the heat and stir sauce until smooth and thickened. Strain the sauce through a fine sieve and set aside to cool.

Place the steak into a baking dish and pour the sauce over. Cover the dish with plastic wrap and marinate in the refrigerator for at least 3 hours (more like 4–6 hours). Drain the steak and discard the marinade. Thread the steak onto bamboo skewers (allow the steak to come up to room temperature before cooking). Preheat the barbecue and cook the kebabs over medium heat until done to your liking. Serve with crusty bread and a crisp green salad. Serves 8.

BARBECUED LAMB
BASQUE STYLE

3 kg leg of lamb, boned

60 mL dry sherry

2 tablespoons olive oil

2 teaspoons dried mixed
   herbs

3 slices bacon

1 teaspoon finely minced
   onion

½ teaspoon rosemary

125 mL tomato sauce

60 mL white wine vinegar

1 cup tomato purée

½ teaspoon salt

1 clove garlic, peeled and
   crushed

250 mL dry white wine

The Basque people are an interesting lot. Uncorroborated, semi-informed sources tell me their language is a complete linguistic anomaly to Europe and certainly to their homeland in northern Spain. Speaking of language, they apparently have more in common with Indo-Chinese groups than with their local European brethren.

They are also crack shepherds and are employed in and around the high mountain pastures of the American west and Rocky Mountain regions. Their characteristic wagons, strikingly similar to the 'gypsy caravans' of the UK and Europe, are seen routinely along the roads of central Idaho and the morning air is often pierced by their unique yodel-like call.

As shepherds, they've honed the task of preparing tasty lamb dishes to a fine art. After trying this barbecue approach, inspired by Basque cookery, I'm sure you'll agree…

In a bowl, combine the sherry, oil and mixed herbs. Place the lamb in a large baking dish and pour the marinade over, turning the meat in the sauce to ensure it's well marinated. Cover the dish tightly with plastic wrap and refrigerate for at least 8 hours, turning the meat from time to time.

Drain the lamb and reserve the marinade.

Lay the bacon slices out on a flat surface and cover with rosemary and onion. Roll each slice up tightly and cut each roll in half to yield six smaller rolls. With a surgically sharp knife, make six deep incisions in the lamb and insert the bacon rolls. Season the lamb with salt and pepper. Reshape the lamb and truss with string.

Place the reserved marinade in a bowl and add the tomato sauce, vinegar, tomato purée, salt, garlic and white wine.

Cook the lamb over medium heat, turning frequently and basting with the marinade mixture for approximately 1½ hours or until it's cooked to your liking. Serve with a green salad, tomato, oregano and vinaigrette salad and crusty bread. Serves 8.

BARBECUED SPATCHCOCK

6 spatchcock

250 mL sherry

125 mL olive oil

1 onion, peeled and minced

1 tablespoon Worcestershire sauce

1 teaspoon light soy sauce

juice of ½ lemon

1 small clove garlic, peeled and crushed

¼ teaspoon dried thyme

¼ teaspoon dried oregano

¼ teaspoon dried marjoram

Spatchcock present an interesting challenge to the barbecue chef. The relative rarity of the species and elimination of their alpine mountain habitat make individuals in the 2–4 kg class abysmally expensive. Their long green tentacles and pearlescent, chitinous outer shell are tough obstacles unless the freshly dispatched and gutted spatchcock are first par-boiled (this also makes pin feather removal much easier).

Another dressing-out tip: Being careful to avoid their needle-like incisors, drive a stout nail through their head and into a large immovable object (such as a tree). Score the skin just above their leathery wattles with a sharp knife. Grasp their fibrous snout firmly with a pair of pliers and pull down in one smooth motion. This method removes the gills, reproductive organs and their silly, 'smart-alecky' grin. Of course, if I had someone score my leathery wattles with a sharp knife, grasp my snout with a pair of pliers and remove my reproductive organs in one smooth downward motion, I wouldn't have much to smile about either!

Now that you've prepared the little critters properly, try this recipe and I personally guarantee that you'll never eat spatchcock any other way!

ONLY KIDDING! Regular spatchcock will do.

In a medium bowl, combine the sherry, oil, onion, Worcestershire sauce, soy sauce, lemon juice, garlic and herbs. Mix like there's no tomorrow.

Place the spatchcock in a baking dish large enough to hold all of them. Pour the marinade over and turn the spatchcock in the sauce so they are well covered. Cover the dish tightly with plastic wrap and refrigerate for at least 2 hours.

Preheat the barbecue. Drain the spatchcock and reserve the marinade. Cook them over medium heat, turning frequently and basting with the marinade, for 20–30 minutes or to your liking. Serves 6.

Spicy Ham Steaks

6 thick-cut ham steaks

60 g unsalted butter, melted

250 mL sherry

250 mL pineapple juice

½ teaspoon ground cloves

1 tablespoon Dijon mustard

2 tablespoons honey

1 teaspoon paprika

1 clove garlic, peeled and crushed

salt and pepper to taste

These ham steaks are perfect for almost any barbecue situation. Once again, your marinade is a key player here, giving the ham its spicy, flavourful character. In this case, spicy doesn't mean 'hot' as in jalapeno, Kenyan chillies, tabasco and certain rust-coloured pyrotechnic liquids locally produced and bottled in Jamaica. It merely means redolent with spices. Being a big supporter of 'high-temperature' comestibles and seeker of indigenous goods that aren't usually exported, I purchased a locally brewed hot sauce while visiting the Caribbean's Cayman Islands. I'm afraid I can't even remember the name of the stuff now, which is a shame since the rest of the story is chemically etched in my brain forever.

I had grilled up some hamburgers with some friends as the sun sank on the azure horizon. Enjoying the soft twilight breezes, I toasted some buns, cut some thick slices of juicy red onion and plump tomato and pulled apart a head of lettuce, getting ready to enjoy some 'bongo' burgers. From the cabinet I produced my vividly decorated flask of 'special sauce'. Being innately adventurous yet cautious, I dabbed a small amount of the pulpy, reddish-brown sauce on my tomato slice and clapped on the top bun. I offered the sauce around, but everyone else decided to pass until they saw my reaction.

We all chowed down and there was a moment of stony silence as everyone looked at me for some sign of approval. It tasted as though I had bitten into a chunk of semi-solid lava! My tastebuds were napalmed! I thought I'd tasted the world's hottest capsicum, munched on jalapenos that made grown men cry, and had curries in England that could have doubled as oil-based paint remover, but I had never tasted anything like that. I reflexively expunged the small bite of burger I'd taken and began consuming prodigious amounts of cheap white bread, vainly attempting to quench the inferno in my mouth. It was months before I had anything spicier than apple sauce!

Spicy Ham Steaks continued

But this ham steak isn't 'hot', it's spicy and there's a BIG difference …

In a bowl, combine the melted butter, sherry, pineapple juice, cloves, mustard, honey, paprika and garlic. Season to taste with salt and pepper. Place the ham steaks in a large flat baking dish and pour the marinade over. Cover the dish with plastic wrap and refrigerate for 1 hour, turning the steaks occasionally.

Preheat the barbecue. Remove the meat from the refrigerator and allow to warm to room temperature (about 10–15 minutes, depending on thickness). Cook the steaks over medium heat for 3–4 minutes or to your liking, brushing each steak with the marinade as you turn them. Serves 6.

PORK SATAYS

500 g pork fillet

1 teaspoon white wine vinegar

2 spring onions, finely chopped

2 tablespoons soy sauce

2 tablespoons honey

2 tablespoons corn oil

Satay Sauce
200 g unsalted peanuts, ground

2 teaspoons corn oil

1 small red chilli, seeded and chopped

1 small onion, peeled and chopped

2 cloves garlic, peeled and crushed

4 teaspoons soy sauce

1 tablespoon honey

juice of ½ lemon

1 tablespoon desiccated coconut

125 mL water

A delectable pork dish that's perfect finger food for summer get-togethers. Satays carry their Asian heritage for fine cuisine that's definitely low-tech yet delicious. Feel free to make satays as a starter for multi-course presentations or as a main course accompanied by steamed rice or Asian noodles for lighter fare. Experiment with the marinade and satay sauce by substituting fruit juices, soy, tamari and oyster sauces, and tabasco or pepper sauce to establish your temperature threshold.

Keep 'em spinning as they grill to ensure even cooking!

Cut the pork into skewer-sized pieces. In a bowl, combine the vinegar, spring onions, soy sauce, honey and oil. Place the pork in a baking dish and pour the marinade over. Cover the dish with plastic wrap and refrigerate for at least 3 hours (better overnight!).

Drain the pork and reserve the marinade. Thread the pork pieces onto bamboo skewers.

To make the sauce: In a heavy-based frying pan, heat the oil over medium heat and add the garlic, onion and chilli and sauté for 2 minutes. Add the peanuts, soy sauce, honey, lemon juice, coconut and water. Season to taste with salt and pepper. Simmer gently over low heat for 4 minutes.

Preheat the barbecue. Cook the satays, brushing liberally with the marinade, for 4–5 minutes or until cooked through. Serve with your 'knockout' satay sauce. Serves 6.

GREEK-STYLE FISH KEBABS

1 kg firm white fish fillets

60 mL olive oil

125 mL dry white wine

juice of 1 lemon

salt and pepper to taste

1 teaspoon dried oregano

1 small clove garlic, peeled and crushed

1 small onion, peeled and finely minced

1 large green capsicum, cored and deseeded

12 bay leaves

12 cherry tomatoes

12 button mushrooms

1 lemon, cut into 6 wedges

Leave it to the Greeks, wizards of simple, nourishing and delectable cookery, to come up with fish kebabs that will turn even the most devout 'meat-and-potatoes' person into a dyed-in-the-wool disciple of aquaculture. Once again, the marinade separates the smelts from the whitebait here! Never rush marinating, call for pizza instead.

In a medium-sized bowl, combine the oil, wine, lemon juice, oregano, garlic and onion. Season to taste with salt and freshly ground black pepper. Cut the fish into bite-sized pieces and place in a deep baking dish. Pour the marinade over, cover dish with plastic wrap and refrigerate for at least 8 hours (how about overnight!?).

Cut the capsicum into 2 cm squares, give or take a few nano-microns. Wipe the mushrooms with a clean, damp cloth (NEVER wash or peel!). Drain the fish and reserve the marinade.

Thread the fish chunks, capsicum, bay leaves, cherry tomatoes and the button mushrooms alternately on bamboo skewers. Preheat the barbecue. Cook the fish kebabs over medium heat, turning and basting with the marinade occasionally, for approximately 6–8 minutes or until cooked to your liking. Serve with herbed rice, pita bread and a bottle of Retsina. (A word of warning: A Retsina hangover is not a pretty sight, take it from personal experience. Use this Hellenic tonic in moderation.) Serves 6.

BARBECUED MARINATED FISH

4 fillets of firm, white, boneless fish

125 mL light soy sauce

250 mL white wine

juice of 1 lemon

2 cloves garlic, peeled and crushed

2 cm fresh ginger root, peeled and grated

125 mL olive oil

2 tablespoons chopped fresh rosemary

6 tablespoons chopped fresh parsley

Long a strictly carnivorous barbecue chef, I've since changed my tune. These days, almost 70 per cent of my backyard banquets focus on finned fare, fish being good value and a healthful crowd pleaser.

Fish with firmer flesh (say that three times, rapidly!) do better on the grill than their delicate, flaky counterparts. Remember to rub the grill area with absorbent kitchen paper soaked in vegetable oil prior to reheating. This helps prevent the flesh from sticking, an especially important function among fish with lower natural oil content.

Try this multi-purpose marinade on that next 'rod-bender' that doesn't get away, or go to the fishmonger and have him toss the fish over the counter so you can truthfully say you caught it! Here's a first 'plaice' winner that'll have you in the 'chips' with friends and family alike!

In a bowl, combine the soy sauce, wine, lemon juice, garlic, ginger and oil. Place the fish in a large, flat baking dish and pour the marinade over. Cover the dish with plastic wrap and refrigerate for at least 3 hours.

Drain the fish and reserve the marinade. Preheat the barbecue. Sprinkle the fish generously with the rosemary and parsley (the stuff is cheap, loosen up!) and place inside a wire fish griller. Place over medium heat and cook each side, basting with the marinade, for approximately 5–7 minutes or until the flesh flakes easily with a fork. Serve with a medley of peas, rice and diced baby carrots. Serves 4.

SEAFOOD KEBABS

1 kg large green prawns

18 large oysters

250 g bacon

4 large tomatoes

18 button onions, peeled

2 green capsicums, cored and deseeded

80 mL light soy sauce

1 onion, peeled and finely chopped

5 cm fresh ginger root, peeled and grated

1 teaspoon French mustard

1 teaspoon horseradish sauce

½ teaspoon cumin

Think of these crowd pleasers as mini-fishmarkets on skewers! Mix and match and experiment with various seafood combinations. In my lifetime, I've only found seven people who claim to not like seafood. And I have good reason to believe that four of them were bluffing! As in all meats, go for the freshest, best looking you can buy. Being particularly delicate, seafood generally suffers the most from deep freezing. I have been told that freezing fish in a container full of water helps preserve the texture and prevents 'freezer burn'. It's worth a try. So's this recipe …

In a bowl, combine the soy sauce, chopped onion, ginger, garlic, mustard, horseradish and cumin. Cover and set aside for 4 hours.

Shell and devein the prawns and place in a baking dish. Pour the marinade over, cover the bowl with plastic wrap and refrigerate for 2 hours.

Blanch the oysters in hot water for a few seconds, then drain and wrap them in strips of bacon and secure with a toothpick. Cut the tomatoes in quarters. Cut the capsicum into kebab-sized pieces. Drain the prawns and reserve the marinade. Thread the seafood, onions and capsicum onto bamboo skewers. Cook the kebabs to your liking, brushing constantly with the marinade. Serves 6.

BARBECUED DUCKLING

2.5 kg duckling

125 mL orange juice

60 mL light soy sauce

1 teaspoon brown sugar

salt and pepper to taste

Duckling, like goose, ordinarily tends to be a bit greasy. But barbecuing (on a spit) can often solve that problem by allowing the fat to drip out as it cooks. Try this duck 'à la Orange Juice' and see if it's not the best you've ever had …

In a bowl, combine the orange juice, soy sauce and brown sugar. Stir until the sugar dissolves. Season to taste with salt and freshly ground pepper. Place mixture in a small saucepan and bring to a low simmer, cooking for 2 minutes.

Preheat your barbecue. Place the trussed duck on the spit and roast slowly for 1–1½ hours, basting with the orange sauce occasionally. Serves 4.

FAMILY MEALS

SHEPHERD'S PIE

500 g premium minced steak

2 onions, peeled and
 chopped

1 tablespoon olive oil

1 tablespoon flour

salt and black pepper
 to taste

250 mL good beef stock

2 teaspoons Worcestershire
 sauce

Topping
750 g potatoes, peeled and
 quartered

40 mL milk

20 g unsalted butter

30 g Cheddar cheese, grated

Apparently there's no connection between Shepherd's Pie and Jean Shepherd, the American humourist. Nor is there any connection to any Shepherds I know. I do know that I virtually existed on the stuff in the 'jolly olde UK' a couple of lifetimes ago. A real stick-to-your-ribs (and virtually every-where else!) kind of dish. Between this and the odd chicken curry, I fended off starvation in the 'Land That Food Forgot'. Eminently more delicious when followed by a pint of bitter, specifically one that, if held to the light, resembles a glass of rusty pond water. Ah! The best!

Place the oil (cold-pressed, extra-virgin) in a heavy-based frying pan over medium heat and sauté the onions until transparency reigns. Add the mince and brown it, crumbling it with a wooden spoon as you go. Remove from the heat and stir in the flour. Salt and pepper to taste. Slowly add the beef stock, stirring copiously, if not feverishly. Add the Worcester-shire sauce and mix well. Return to the heat and bring to the boil. Reduce heat and simmer gently or until the meat is tender (approximately 25 minutes). If the meat begins quoting Shelley, Byron or Keats, it's done!

Boil the potatoes in a large pan of salted water until tender (see 19th-century British romantics, above). Drain. Add the milk and butter to the pan. Mash the potatoes well and season to taste with salt and freshly ground black pepper.

Preheat the oven to 180°C.

Place the mince mixture into the bottom of a deep pie dish and top with the mashed potatoes. Level the top with a fork. If not absolutely level, saw portions of your workbench's legs off to compensate. (Only kidding, just wanted to see if you were still following the directions.) Sprinkle with grated cheese. Bake in the oven for 10–15 minutes or until the cheese is golden brown and the pie heated through. Serves 4 (shepherds, without sheep).

MEXICAN VEAL CUTLETS

4 boned veal cutlets

1 onion, peeled and sliced

1 green capsicum, cored
and sliced

1 clove garlic, peeled and
crushed

300 mL chicken stock

300 mL milk

2 egg yolks, lightly beaten

salt and pepper to taste

1 tablespoon olive oil

125 g grated tasty cheese

I named this dish after having it immediately upon my return from Mexico. Otherwise it has little to do with that, magnificent country. Oh yes, there is a green capsicum involved here, as well as grated cheese, but otherwise it's merely a hearty way to prepare veal cutlets with an intriguing blend of garlic and spices. When your family and friends begin to chant "Not veal cutlets again!", unleash this one and see if they don't fall strangely silent...

Preheat the oven to 180°C.

Heat the oil (cold-pressed, extra-virgin) in a heavy-based frying pan. Add the cutlets, onions, capsicum and garlic. Sauté quickly until the cutlets are uniformly browned but not totally cooked through. Transfer vegetables and meat to a baking dish using a slotted spoon.

In a small saucepan, combine the milk and chicken stock. Bring to the boil and reduce heat to simmer until the liquid begins to thicken. Remove from the heat and cool slightly. Stir in the egg yolks and mix thoroughly. Pour this mixture over the cutlets. Bake in the oven for 30–40 minutes or until the cutlets are cooked and the sauce is a golden brown colour. Sprinkle the dish with grated cheese and place under a hot grill or browning element in the oven until the cheese has melted to a golden brown. Serve with buttered noodles and a Mexican salad. Serves 4 (or less).

HEARTY VEAL STEW

750 g stewing veal

30 g plain flour

salt and freshly ground
   black pepper to taste

8 button onions, peeled

4 carrots, scraped and cut
   into 5 cm lengths

2 stalks celery, sliced

16 button mushrooms

1 tablespoon unsalted butter

1 tablespoon olive oil

150 mL chicken stock

150 mL white wine

300 mL milk

1 tablespoon chopped
   parsley

When in doubt, make stew! They're easy to make and probably the most forgiving of dishes. If you can heat water, you can make stew. And unless you start with 'pet food-grade' meat, it'll taste like a million dollars. In this case we're using veal, delicately flavoured and very tender. The secret ingredient here is the chicken stock in combination with the white wine. A stew with class. What can I say?

Cut the veal into bite-sized pieces (this is a relative term, size the cuts to the anticipated consuming mouths). Place the flour, salt and pepper into a large, clean brown paper bag (remove all till receipts, spare change and house keys!). Place the veal, a few pieces at a time, in the bag and shake vigorously to coat with the seasoned flour mixture. Wipe the mushrooms with a clean, damp cloth (NEVER wash or peel!).

Heat the butter and oil in a large, heavy-based saucepan. When the butter foam begins to subside, add the meat and onions and brown on all sides. Slowly add the chicken stock, wine and milk and stir gently to combine.

Bring to the boil, reduce heat and simmer for approximately 2 minutes or until the liquid begins to thicken. Add the carrots, celery and mushrooms. Season to taste with salt and pepper. Bring back to the boil, reduce heat, cover and simmer very gently until meat is tender (approximately 2 hours). Serve with mashed potatoes. Serves 4 (or so).

MARK'S FAMOUS MEATBALLS

500 g minced veal

2 medium-size eggs, beaten

1 thick slice bread, crusts
  removed

zest of one lemon

1 clove garlic, peeled and
  crushed

2 tablespoons chopped
  parsley

1 tablespoon milk

30 g unsalted butter

salt and freshly ground
  black pepper to taste

These are the meatballs that 'Won the West'. These little babies have caused family feuds to cease, placated losses in love and repaired shattered egos when huge trout have squirmed free from grasping hands or ill-handled nets. The secret to success with these mince masterpieces lies in two major components: the veal (buy the best you can) and the attitude with which you prepare them. Whipped up in a fury or in depression, for some reason they taste extra-ordinarily average. But orchestrate them in a buoyant, joyful, 'up' frame of mind and you'll have people ransoming your dog for the recipe. I haven't a clue how it works, it just does! Give 'em a go…

In a bowl, combine the veal mince, lemon zest, parsley and garlic. Soak the bread in the milk, then add it to the mince with the beaten egg. Season to taste with salt and pepper. Mix well to combine ingredients. With floured hands, shape the mince into meatballs and place on a greased baking tray.

(Note: activities to avoid with floured hands include answering the telephone, handling navy-blue cashmere blazers, operating expensive stereo equipment, tying salmon or trout flies and visiting the gents!)

When all the meatballs are made, cover the tray with plastic wrap and refrigerate for 30 minutes.

Melt the butter in a heavy-based frying pan. When the butter foam subsides, fry the meatballs, turning them as they cook, for approximately 7–10 minutes or until cooked through. Serve with your favourite pasta in a hearty red tomato sauce and a bottle of Chianti. Serves 4 (depending on sauce and pasta!).

MARINATED LAMB CHOPS

12 lamb loin chops

juice of 1 large lemon

1 tablespoon olive oil

1 clove garlic, crushed

1 tablespoon chopped
parsley

1 teaspoon dried rosemary

salt and freshly ground
black pepper to taste

At first glance, you'd think that lamb wouldn't take well to marinating, but not so! This dish proves that the subtle yet distinct flavour of lamb is actually *enhanced* by marinating. Go for the best lamb chops you can buy. Why save pennies, then suffer through an intensely average meal? Get to know your butcher, if you don't already. By the way, buy from a butcher whenever you can. Supermarkets put you 'too far away' from the meat. By the time you get it, it's generally shrink-wrapped on poly foam and starting to head rapidly downhill. When you buy from a human being who depends on repeat and loyal customers for business survival, you're bound to get better service and better meat. But we were talking about lamb chops. Here's a tasty way of preparing them that I guarantee you'll swear by, not at!

Start with a sharp knife (is there any other kind?) and carefully trim as much visible fat off the chops as possible. Place them in a baking dish. In a small bowl, combine the lemon juice, oil (cold-pressed, extra-virgin), garlic, parsley, rosemary and season with salt and pepper. Pour this marinade over the chops. Cover the dish with plastic wrap and place in the refrigerator for at least 2 hours (more like half a day!).

Rub grill surface with a small amount of oil and preheat. Remove the chops from the marinade and grill on both sides to your taste. Remember: Try diligently to strike a balance between lamb sushi and lamb à la carbon. Serve with buttered new baby potatoes and minted peas. Serves 6 (polite diners).

IRISH STEW

1 kg neck lamb chops

2 kg potatoes

2 large onions, peeled and
  sliced

salt and freshly ground
  black pepper

625 mL water

1 tablespoon chopped fresh
  parsley

¼ teaspoon dried thyme

2 bay leaves

I know you'll enjoy this easy-to-prepare, hearty stew as much as I do. Lamb plays a leading role with vegies holding strong supporting parts. Great for winter evenings, preferably in the vicinity of a real fireplace, burning real wood, drinking real beer. Serve with rolls to aid plate cleaning! Once again, don't look for left-over containers too diligently…you won't need 'em!

Preheat the oven to 180°C.

Peel the potatoes and slice thickly. Trim all the visible fat from the lamb chops. Place a layer of sliced potato in the bottom of a casserole. Place the chops on top. Sprinkle with the parsley and thyme. Add the bay leaves and salt and pepper to taste, then layer the rest of the potatoes over them. Add the water and cover the casserole tightly. Cook in the oven until the meat is tender, approximately 2 hours. Serves 6 (4 Irish Stew lovers).

Pork and Chickpea Casserole

500 g pork leg steak, cut in 1 piece

1 tablespoon olive oil

1 large onion, peeled and chopped

2 cloves garlic, peeled and crushed

4 rashers bacon, chopped

1 small red capsicum, chopped

1 cup tomato paste

½ teaspoon chilli powder

salt and black pepper to taste

1 cup cooked chickpeas

125 mL cider vinegar

Pork and chickpeas! Why not? After all, we're talking cooking, not world disarmament! The much-maligned chickpea performs yeoman's work in a number of culinary capacities, being both tasty and nutritious.

Aside from this recipe, my personal favourite application of the blessed Garbanzo bean is the lustily fragrant falafel, a fast-food fantasy comprised of golf ball-sized, spicy spheres of mashed chickpeas, redolent with paprika and garlic, deep-fried and served in an open pita or Middle Eastern pocket bread' with lettuce and tahini dressing. I initially ran across this lunchtime legend several years ago while working in New York. Unfortunately, not unlike other examples of disappearing flora and fauna, non-toxic falafel is becoming increasingly difficult to find on the streets of Manhattan (from roving food vendors, with trolleys actually, not lying at the kerb!). If I had but a 10-cent piece for every afternoon meeting that was 'nuked' by the odd irresponsibly consumed falafel, I wouldn't be forced to write cookbooks for a living. But let's get back to the recipe…

Using the sharpest knife you can lay your hands on (continually sharpen them), cut the pork into bite-sized pieces. In a heavy-based frying pan, heat the oil (cold-pressed, extra-virgin) over medium heat. When oil is hot (smell it, don't use your finger!) add the diced pork and brown on all sides. Remove pork with a slotted spoon and drain on absorbent kitchen paper.

Add the onions, garlic, bacon and capsicum to the pan, cooking all the ingredients until the onions are translucent. Add the tomato paste, chilli powder, vinegar, browned pork and the drained chickpeas. Season to taste with salt and pepper. Put on some funky reggae tunes and 'stir it up'.

Cover the pan, bring to the boil, reduce heat and simmer very gently until pork is tender, approximately 1–2 hours (depending on your pork!). Serve with crisp green salad and crusty bread. Serves 4 (friends or relatives).

SPECIAL SPAGHETTI BOLOGNESE

500 g best minced steak

2 tablespoons olive oil

1 large onion, peeled and chopped

1 clove garlic, peeled and crushed

1 stalk celery, sliced

1 small red capsicum, cored and chopped

1 small green capsicum, cored and chopped

250 mL good beef stock

125 mL red wine

3 tablespoon tomato purée

salt and freshly ground black pepper to taste

300 g spaghetti

What's so special about this recipe? I got it from an Indian chap I shared a train car with once in Athens. This one elevates spaghetti to intoxicating new heights of gustatory pleasure. It doesn't taste too bad either! Be forewarned: Be prepared to share this recipe with friends, relatives and anyone else you invite to sit at your table. Do what I do and have the instructions transcribed and photocopied for easy distribution. I have no idea where the Indian chap got it!

Heat the oil (cold-pressed, extra-virgin) in a heavy-based saucepan and add the garlic, onions, celery and capsicum over medium heat until the onions are transparent. If no one is looking, add extra garlic. If someone is looking, crane your neck toward the nearest window and say (for women): "I'd swear that was Mel Gibson in a loincloth!" (for men): "Wow! You don't see that many Ferrari 330-GT cabriolets around here any more … especially not with naked women drivers!" As they dash to the window, add more garlic.

Add the mince and brown it, crumbling the meat with a wooden spoon as it cooks. Add the tomato purée, beef stock, red wine and season to taste with salt and pepper. Stir well to combine all ingredients. Bring the sauce to the boil, reduce heat and simmer gently until the meat is tender, approximately 1 hour.

Boil the spaghetti in a large pan of lightly salted water, adding just a splash of olive oil before plunging the pasta in. Cook spaghetti until *al dente*, according to the directions on the packet! Note: Never rinse the spaghetti! It washes away all the good stuff!

Serve with sauce on individual serving plates and sprinkle with Parmesan or Romano cheese. Good with a green salad and garlic or plain crusty bread. Serves 4 (2 big-time pasta pros).

LAMB CUTLETS MEDITERRANEAN-STYLE

60 g fresh breadcrumbs

60 g finely chopped ham

salt and freshly ground
  black pepper

30 g flour

6 large lamb cutlets

1 egg, lightly beaten

2 tomatoes, skinned and
  chopped

1 red capsicum, cored and
  sliced

1 onion, peeled and
  chopped

3 tablespoons butter

1 teaspoon paprika

1 teaspoon tomato purée

1 tablespoon chopped
  parsley

If they didn't invent lamb in the Mediterranean, they certainly refined it to an art! Many of my favourite Greek dishes are lamb-based, rich and spicy with lamb's unique flavour and texture. There's really nothing like it! Here's a real winner for us lamb lovers that's a breeze to make and a treat to eat! Enjoy!

Pour the breadcrumbs into a bowl and add the ham. Sprinkle the flour on a large flat plate and season with salt and pepper. Coat the cutlets with the seasoned flour, dip them into the beaten egg mixture and coat them with the breadcrumbs and ham, pressing the coating on well without making a mess that takes a team of five to clean up. Place the cutlets on a flat dish, cover with plastic wrap and chill in the fridge for 30 minutes.

Melt half the butter in a heavy-based saucepan. Add the onions and cook until they're transparent (if you can read the evening newspaper through them, they're done!). Add the tomato purée, tomatoes and capsicum. Season to taste with salt and pepper. Bring to the boil, reduce heat and simmer gently for 3–4 minutes.

Melt the remaining butter in a large, heavy-based frying pan over medium heat. Fry the cutlets in the butter until golden brown. Arrange the cutlets on individual serving dishes and pour a little of the tomato sauce over them. Sprinkle with chopped parsley and serve with cauliflower and green beans. Serves 6 (if two are slimming).

Marinated Pork Chops

4 pork loin chops

2 carrots, scraped and sliced

1 onion, peeled and sliced

1 bay leaf

2 teaspoons chopped
parsley

1 clove garlic, peeled and
crushed

¼ teaspoon dried rosemary

350 mL white wine

60 g unsalted butter

1 teaspoon paprika

30 g plain flour

salt and freshly ground
black pepper

I've often said a good marinade makes average meat tasty and a good meat truly outstanding. Here's an opportunity to experiment with pork chops and a white wine-based marinade that will hook even the most finicky guests. Don't scrimp on your marinade base! If it's wine, buy good wine. If it's beer, buy good beer. Rule of thumb: Never cook with an alcoholic beverage you wouldn't drink from a glass. Actually, the quality is even more critical in cooking because the alcohol vaporises almost immediately when heated, so you're left with the essence of the liquid. If you start with bad liquid, you'll be left with bad essence. Sounds vaguely metaphysical, doesn't it?

Lay the pork chops in a large baking dish. In a bowl combine the carrots, onions, bay leaf, parsley, garlic, rosemary and wine. Stir well, in fact, stir better than you've ever stirred before! Pour this mixture over the chops. Cover the dish, refrigerate and let the marinade 'do its thing' for at least 8–12 hours.

Remove the chops from the fridge and drain, reserving the marinade. Melt the butter in a heavy-based frying pan and when the foam begins to subside add the drained chops and brown on all sides. Gingerly remove the browned chops from the pan and reserve in a warm dish. Stir the flour into the remaining butter in the pan and cook (without burning!) for 1 minute. Remove from the heat and slowly add the remaining marinade, stirring continuously.

Return the pan to the heat and bring to the boil, stirring constantly. Reduce heat, return the chops to the pan and simmer very gently for approximately 20 minutes. Add the paprika and simmer for a further 5 minutes or until the chops are tender. Serve with steamed cabbage, mashed potatoes and carrots. Serves 4 (moderate eaters).

CHILLI CON CARNE

1 kg best minced steak

2 large onions, peeled and chopped

3 tablespoons olive oil

2 cloves garlic, peeled and crushed

1 teaspoon chilli powder or to taste

1 teaspoon cumin powder

125 mL water

1 cup tomato purée

1 x 440 g can peeled tomatoes

salt and freshly ground black pepper

1 x 440 g can red kidney beans

Chilli is a dish near and dear to my heart. It's where I got my start. The way I eat chilli, it almost qualifies as substance abuse!

Like most 'addicts', I started experimenting with chilli when I was a youngster, when I didn't know any better. As I grew older I thought I was King! I thought I could handle it. Sure, I ate a lot of chilli, even for breakfast, but hey! It was 'hip',

Besides, it wasn't as though I NEEDED chilli! I could give it up any time. Hell, sometimes I went two, nearly three days without having any. Then even I started noticing strange, dysfunctional chilli behaviours. I would sneak chilli into my bedroom, under my bed, for a 'nightcap'. I was taking it with me in the car for even short trips around town. Then I was bringing it to the office in plastic tubs 'just in case of emergencies'. I was headed for trouble, even my best friends were telling me so, but I wouldn't (or couldn't) listen.

Pretty soon it was out of hand. I needed my daily chilli 'fix' or I was unbearable to be around (come to think of it, I was pretty unbearable to be around anyway!). Chilli began to run my life. While on the road, I stopped in every bar and coffee shop that served chilli. What's worse, I was reaching natural resistance levels where two, three 'hits' a day weren't enough to satisfy my craving. Even today, as a recovering chilli-aholic, one bowl, garnished with boiled rice and small crackers, I know will put me over the edge. Try this chilli at your own risk…

Heat the oil (cold-pressed, extra-virgin) in a heavy-based saucepan over medium heat. Add the onions and garlic and cook until the onions are transparent. Add the chilli powder and cumin, continue cooking for another minute or so.

Add the mince to the pan and brown it, crumbling it with a wooden spoon as it browns. Add the water (try substituting beer!), tomato purée and undrained tomatoes and stir feverishly to combine. Season with salt and pepper. Bring to the boil, reduce heat and simmer for 30 minutes (ideally it should be simmered 2–3 days, but this is seldom practical).

Drain the kidney beans and add to the pot, cooking for an additional 10 minutes or until the mince melts in your mouth. Pour the chilli into a large serving bowl and serve with boiled rice and plenty of cold beer.   Serves 6 (light eaters).

CHICKEN AND CAPSICUM CASSEROLE

1 kg chicken joints, thighs and legs

6 medium-sized potatoes, peeled and cut into bite-sized pieces

2 tablespoons olive oil

150 mL white wine

salt and freshly ground black pepper

60 g unsalted butter

4 medium-sized, evenly shaped red capsicums

Chicken and capsicum are a natural combination. The colours work, the flavours crackle and it's good for you too! Chicken is the real journeyman in my menu planning. From big 'sit-down' dinners to casual buffets, chicken 'struts its stuff' as tasty, healthful fare. This recipe incorporates roasted capsicum, a food fit for the gods. This delight also separates the 'Real Cooks' from the 'Real Men' because so much energy and effort is needed. If available, I heartily suggest that you buy the already-roasted variety, usually packed in olive oil and a little vinegar and spices. This will save you approximately 25 'Real Man' hours in the menu development department. Try this, you'll like it …

Place the chicken in a large baking dish. In a small bowl combine the oil (cold-pressed, extra-virgin) and white wine and pour over the chicken. Cover the dish and allow to marinate in the refrigerator for 30 minutes to 1 hour.

Preheat the oven to 200°C. Remove the cover from the baking dish, add the potatoes and bake in the oven for 15 minutes. Remove from the oven and add the butter.

When the butter melts, baste the joints with the dish juices. Return to the oven and continue cooking for a further 30 minutes.

Meanwhile, preheat the grill to 'hot'. Wash the capsicum and pat dry with absorbent kitchen paper. Place under a hot grill (the capsicum, not the absorbent paper!) and cook, rotating them frequently, until the skins are blackened. Remove from the grill and plunge them into ice-cold water (the roasted capsicum, not you!). Drain and peel, removing the flesh from the core and cutting into strips.

Add the capsicum strips to the chicken casserole and continue to bake for an additional 15 minutes. At the end of the cooking time, carefully remove the dish and allow to cool slightly. Serve right from the dish, accompanied by boiled potatoes and zucchini. Serves 6 (or thereabouts).

BEEF AND BEER CASSEROLE

750 g best stewing steak

60 g plain flour

salt and freshly ground
  black pepper

2 medium onions, peeled
  and chopped

30 g unsalted butter

1 tablespoon olive oil

375 mL beer

125 mL good beef stock

2 teaspoons Dijon mustard

1 teaspoon sugar

1 teaspoon salt, extra

1 large bay leaf

Cooking with beer allegedly goes back to the 9th century, when an errant shepherd (see Shepherd's Pie) accidentally knocked his mug o' suds into his supper pot. Although grief-stricken by the loss of his brew, the shepherd was delighted with the new depth and texture of his soaked mouldy bread stew and a trend was born. Experiment with different brands of lager, ale and bitter to achieve hops-oriented nirvana!

Preheat the oven to 180°C.

Cut the steak into bite-sized pieces. Not shredded mouthfuls, bite-sized pieces! Place 60 g of flour into a large clean brown paper bag. Please remove all discount coupons, product hang-tags, spare change and till receipts – unfortunately they are non-nutritional. Season with salt and freshly ground pepper. Drop the steak in the bag, a few pieces at a time, and shake it up. Any album by James Brown serves as an excellent shaking soundtrack. Coat all beef evenly and remove from the bag. Now throw away the meat, eat the bag and… ONLY KIDDING!

Heat the butter and oil (cold-pressed, extra-virgin) in a heavy-based frying pan. When the foam subsides, add the meat carefully and quickly brown evenly over medium heat. Remove from the pan with a slotted spoon and drain on paper towels. Place the meat in a casserole.

Sauté the onions in the pan until transparent. Add the beer (again exercise strict quality control by sampling at each stage), stock, mustard, sugar, salt and bay leaf. Bring to the boil, stirring, and reduce heat and simmer for 4 minutes. Pour over the meat in the casserole. Cover and bake in the oven for approximately 1½ hours or until the meat is tender. Serve with boiled new potatoes, whole baby corn and brussels sprouts. Serves 4 (3 beer drinkers).

SPANISH-STYLE CHICKEN

6 chicken joints, thighs
  and legs

30 g plain flour

salt and freshly ground
  black pepper

60 g unsalted butter

2 tablespoons olive oil

12 button onions, peeled

10 g plain flour, extra

300 mL good chicken stock

40 mL white wine

2 tablespoons tomato purée

300 g thin sausages

1½ cups peas

2 tablespoons chopped
  parsley

Spain – country of romance, adventure and lots of good eating. Spain's on my list of 'must-see' places, a list I hope seriously diminishes pending the publication of a few more zillion-sellers. The irrepressible chicken rides once again with this zesty, family-pleasing dinner. For sausages, look to a Mediterranean or European-style delicatessen or gourmet shop for legitimate Chorizos or a reasonable substitute.

Preheat the oven to 180°C.

Season the 30 g of flour with salt and freshly ground pepper. Coat each chicken joint with the flour. Heat the butter and oil (cold-pressed, extra-virgin) in a large heavy-based frying pan over medium heat. When the foam subsides, add the chicken joints and fry on both sides until golden brown. Remove daintily from the pan and drain on paper towels.

Brown the button onions in the frying pan, then remove with a slotted spoon. Place the onions in the bottom of a casserole and place the chicken on top.

Sprinkle the extra flour into the frying pan and cook, stirring for 1 minute. Don't let that flour burn! Remove from the heat and add the chicken stock, white wine and tomato purée. Mix like a madman to combine. Promptly pour this mixture over the chicken in the casserole. Cover the casserole and bake in the oven for 50 minutes.

Grill the sausages and carefully cut into small pieces. It is a wise idea to cook your sausages several hours ahead of time, allow them to cool in the fridge and then cut them. This will save squirting fat and burned fingers. Boil the peas in salted water for 4 minutes. Drain. Remove the casserole from the oven and cook a further 10 minutes or until the chicken is tender. Or at least non-combative.

Remove from the oven and sprinkle with fresh chopped parsley. Serve with saffron rice and a tossed green salad. Serves 6 (for the most part).

PRAWN FRIED RICE

300 g green prawns, peeled and deveined

4 rashers of bacon

2 cups cooked long-grain rice

1 teaspoon salt

2 large eggs

1 tablespoon olive oil

1 teaspoon of freshly grated root ginger

1 clove garlic, peeled and crushed

6 spring onions, chopped

½ cup cooked peas

1 tablespoon soy sauce or to taste

salt and freshly ground black pepper

The better the prawns, the better the prawn fried rice! Some folks go for the tinned variety or even the freeze-dried version, but not me! I like 'em medium-sized and I like 'em fresh. Leave the prawns big enough to put saddles on to Paul Hogan's 'barbie'. Put your money in the best, freshest mediums you can find. Always go to a fishmonger you can trust and if you don't live near a good fishmonger, move! What's keeping you in that neighbourhood anyway?

Using a wok (first choice) or heavy-based frying pan (distant second), fry the bacon until crisp and golden brown. Remove from the pan and drain on paper towels. Crack the eggs into a mixing bowl and whisk until well blended. Season with salt and pepper. Pour into the pan and cook until set. Gently lift the edge of the omelette from the pan, roll it on a chopping board and slice evenly.

Heat the olive oil in the pan and add the garlic, ginger and spring onion, cooking over medium heat until the onion softens. Add the prawns and cook until they change to a pink colour. Add the rice, increase the heat and stir stridently, frequently tossing with a spatula and cook for approximately 5 minutes, until it is golden. Add the bacon, egg slices, peas and soy sauce and cook, again tossing the rice mixture until the entire dish is heated through. Transfer to a large, warmed serving bowl and serve immediately, garnished with fresh slices of lime. Serves 4 (or 3 and 2 of Paul Hogan's prawns).

Coq-Au-Vin (kawk-aw-van)

6 chicken joints, thighs
  and legs

2 cloves garlic, peeled and
  crushed

¼ teaspoon dried marjoram

400 mL red wine

30 g plain flour

salt and freshly ground
  black pepper

3 tablespoons unsalted
  butter

1 bay leaf

1 tablespoon chopped
  parsley

12 button mushrooms

12 button onions, peeled

4 rashers bacon, chopped

Another French classic! A journeyman in the memorable meal circuit. This dish has, single-handedly, led to more on-the-spot wedding proposals than I can shake a stick at. Imagine! I'm still a young man! Combine chicken and a good hearty Burgundy or Bordeaux and you have a culinary classic. This is a true 'launch-on-warning' dish. If prepared properly, it will invariably succeed when chocolates, long-stemmed roses, Sinatra and taking out the trash without being asked has failed miserably. Try it! Call me collect if it doesn't work … on second thought, call my publisher if it doesn't work!

Place the chicken joints in a large flat baking dish. Combine the wine, garlic and marjoram and pour over the chicken joints. Cover the dish with plastic wrap and marinate in the refrigerator for at least 3–4 hours.

Preheat the oven to 180°C.

Remove the chicken joints from the marinade and reserve the marinade. Dry the chicken joints on paper towels. Place the flour on a large flat plate and season with salt and pepper. Coat the chicken joint liberally with the flour.

Heat the butter in a heavy-based frying pan, adding the chicken and browning it evenly. Remove with a slotted spoon and place in a large casserole. Brown the button onions in the remaining butter and add them to the casserole. Wipe the mushrooms with a clean damp cloth (NEVER WASH) and add to the casserole with the chopped bacon, parsley, bay leaf and marinade.

Cover the casserole and cook in the oven until the chicken is tender, approximately 1 hour. Serve with steamed potatoes, carrots or brussels sprouts. Serves 6 (unsteamed).

MOUSSAKA (moos-ah-kah)

2 small eggplants, sliced

60 mL olive oil

1 tablespoon butter

2 large onions, peeled and
 sliced

400 g cooked lamb,
 chopped

2 tablespoons tomato purée

1 clove garlic, peeled and
 crushed

$1/_8$ teaspoon nutmeg

salt and pepper

4 boiled potatoes, sliced

3 large tomatoes, peeled
 and sliced

Béchamel sauce
1 tablespoon butter

2 tablespoons flour

375 mL milk

salt and pepper

Topping
40 g grated Cheddar cheese

A Greek stand-by. A tasty treat in any language. Many a moussaka bit the dust between my friends and I over innumerable lunches at zillions of Greek coffee shops in Manhattan! Contrary to popular belief, moose meat is not an ingredient! It does, however, include one of the three best things in the world – eggplant. (I'll let you figure out what the other two are!) Try this for an 'international' evening: Serve with Turkish delight for dessert and watch the fireworks.

Lay the sliced eggplant in a large flat dish and sprinkle with salt. Cover with plastic wrap and set aside for 30 minutes. Heat the oil (cold-pressed, extra-virgin) in a heavy-based frying pan and fry the eggplant on both sides until golden brown. Remove from the pan and dry on absorbent kitchen paper.

Melt the butter in the frying pan and sauté the onions and garlic until transparent. Add the lamb, tomato purée, nutmeg and season to taste with salt and pepper. Simmer gently for 3–4 minutes.

Place the meat mixture, in a single layer, in a large baking dish. Next add the layers of tomato, potato and finally the eggplant slices.

Preheat the oven to 180°C.

To make the *béchamel* sauce: Melt the butter in a saucepan and stir in the flour. Cook over a gentle heat for one minute then remove from the heat entirely. Slowly stir in the milk and season to taste with salt and pepper. Return to the heat, bring to the boil, reduce the heat and simmer until the sauce has the consistency of thickened cream.

Pour the sauce over the eggplant. Top with the cheese and bake in the oven for 45 minutes. Serve with crusty bread and a Greek salad. Serves 4 (non-Greeks).

FLO'S FAMOUS EGGPLANT

Some surfers search for the perfect wave, some fishermen cast for the world's record salmon, some people dream of hearing Eric Clapton play 'Layla' just once before they die. Me, I'm searching for the ultimate Eggplant Parmigiana, preferably served as a 'hero' sandwich (on a narrow hard roll).

Over the years I've eaten a lot of bad eggplant, a lot of average eggplant and some outstanding eggplant, but I've never tasted anything like Flo Lewis's eggplant. Flo Lewis is a legend in Boonton, New Jersey, USA. Her house is a registered shrine in the Eggplant Hall of Fame yearbook. And her coffee pot hasn't cooled down in 37 years (when the family took a brief trip to Asbury Park).

Flo Lewis also happens to be Jim Lewis's mum. Jim Lewis is my friend of friends, me high school 'china', my psychic twin and 'soul brother'. Spending a lot of my formative and post-formative years in Flo's kitchen, I knew I had to include Flo's eggplant recipe.

Now Flo's recipe represents a veritable apogee of eggplant on earth, but it can be a bit daunting because Flo has little use for precise measurements or specific instructions. Cooking is a very 'seat-of-the-pants' exercise for her, but it works because she's got that special something that all master chefs possess: 'Invisible Touch'. 'Invisible Touch' is the innate ability to feel, to sense what's right, to know exactly how much of this or that to put in and at what time. People without it struggle for years, scrupulously following recipes, measuring ingredients to the nearest 10th of a gram and having their oven calibrated monthly. But they never reach where Flo is, smiling and waving.

Note: You will soon realise that there are no exact measurements (i.e. of Eggplant, kg, of mozzarella, etc.) in the following recipe. That is because Flo just puts lots of everything in each batch of eggplant she makes. Her motto: ''You buy a lot, you make a lot and you eat a lot.''

Therefore, it's very important that you have several glass casserole or deep baking dishes at the ready to contain all of the 'Flo's Eggplant' you are about to make. Remember, the beauty of this recipe is that it can be frozen and eaten by future generations! With 'Flo's Eggplant' there's no such thing as 'too much'.

1. Get a lot of eggplants (2–3) per available casserole dish. Peel the skin. "Nobody likes the skin," says Flo. Then slice the eggplant into 'very thin' round slices.

2. Break 'several' eggs into a bowl and beat them into a frenzy.

3. Fill another bowl with either breadcrumbs or crushed cornflakes.

4. Cover a flat baking sheet with a 'thin' layer of 'good' olive oil.

5. Heat the oven to 325°F (160°C – Flo generally cooks in Fahrenheit only).

6. Dip the eggplant slices into the beaten eggs, then into the bowl of crumbs. Now lay the eggplant slices on the greased pan. When the pan is full, put it in the oven to bake. After 5 minutes (or when the slices are golden brown), flip them over.

7. Heat some tomato sauce.

8. Grate a 'hunk' (the more the better) of mozzarella cheese.

9. Remove the eggplant from the oven and place on paper towels (this absorbs excess oil).

10. Pour a layer of tomato sauce into a casserole dish. Place a layer of prepared eggplant on this, then a layer of grated mozzarella cheese atop. Alternate layers until the dish is full, and top with 'lots' of mozzarella (leave room at the top so it doesn't spill over when baked).

Keep doing this until you've used up all your ingredients and eggplant. Put aluminium foil over those dishes you wish to save and stick them in the freezer.

To cook, put the uncovered casserole dish in the oven, heated to 350°F (approximately 175°C), and bake for about 30 minutes or until the cheese on top is slightly burned.

ESCALOPES OF VEAL WITH SPIRITED SAUCE

4 large veal escalopes

1 tablespoon olive oil

2 onions, peeled and sliced

80 mL cold water

2 tablespoons cream

2 egg yolks

40 mL brandy

40 mL port

salt and freshly ground
  black pepper to taste

4 slices white bread,
  fried in butter

Warning: With egg yolks, cream and fried bread as important components, this dish is so rich it needs to file a tax return! Prepare this baby annually or on special occasions, as there are enough calories here to sustain a marching army in the Arctic.

What with the liberal doses of brandy and port involved, we also need to remember that cooking successfully with alcohol demands a somewhat disciplined and rock-steady hand in the kitchen. This is especially true with fortified wines and spirits. As the alcohol content or 'proof' of your libations increase, the less frequently you should engage in active 'quality control'. Successful cooking involves sharp knives and extreme heat (electricity or gas) and also requires that the chef be on his toes and unimpaired by excessive alcohol.

If your judgement becomes less than razor sharp thanks to alcohol, not only do you risk serious injury but your food will taste awful! A real calamity! Cuts and severe burns heal, but bad meals are remembered for years.

A word on fried bread. Any 'Real Man' who wishes to avoid becoming a 'Real Cadaver' in the near future will do well to keep this leaden treat at arm's length. I'm not sure who invented fried bread but I've a feeling its roots reach to England, where from ample, first-hand bed-and-breakfast experience, I can tell you this cardiologist's nightmare flourishes today.

I tend to do a lot of trading off in my dietary life and I can't speak for you, but I'd gladly give fried bread a miss and have the odd bowl of ice-cream to fulfil my saturated fat quota. Unless, of course, you don't mind having a cholesterol count that resembles a major stockmarket average. PS: Write me into your will!

Heat the oil (cold-pressed, extra-virgin) in a heavy-based frying pan. Add the veal and onions and cook, turning occasionally, until golden brown.

Escalopes of Veal with Spirited Sauce continued

(Note: When recipes say 'golden brown' always keep to the golden side of the phrase. By the time it reaches brown, it's probably ruined!)

Stir in the water and season to taste with salt and pepper. Reduce heat and simmer very gently for approximately 5–8 minutes. Place the pieces of fried bread in a serving dish. Once the veal has cooked to your taste, remove the escalopes and place one on each slice of fried bread. Set aside but keep warm. Pour the cream into a bowl and stir in the lightly beaten egg yolks, brandy and port. Add this to the gravy in the pan and cook gently, stirring constantly until the sauce begins to thicken. Pour over the escalopes and serve with steamed vegetables and rice. Serves 4 (approximately).

CHICKEN ENCHILADAS

12 corn tortillas

12 black olives, stoned and chopped

180 g Cheddar cheese, grated

Tomato sauce
2 tablespoons olive oil

2 onions, finely chopped

1 clove garlic, peeled and crushed

450 g tomatoes, peeled and chopped

375 mL water

½ packet enchilada sauce mix

salt and freshly ground black pepper to taste

Filling
500 g cooked chopped chicken

300 mL light sour cream

2 tablespoons chopped chives

1 teaspoon chilli powder or to taste

Mexican food has come of age! From 'South of the Border' comes a whole new attitude toward spices, tortillas (tor-tee-yahs) and the beloved jalapeno. Prepared properly, Mexican dishes are nutritious, tasty and easy-easy-easy!

Since I like my food fairly incendiary, I custom-tune most dishes with a heavy hand to the chilli powder, jalapeno and tabasco. Some folks say this is evidence of latent masochism but I prefer the theory recently proposed by some leading neuro-biochemists. An in-depth study apparently indicated that for some people very spicy foods trigger the release of a naturally produced opiate in the brain. Similar to a runner's physiological response to produce endorphins, which in turn produces what's known as the 'runner's high', spicy food instigates a similar response among us culinary 'firemouths'.

When making your 'Mex', keep in mind that presenting it too spicy for your Auntie Irene is as bad as making it too tame for your Uncle Ernie. Adjust the flame to your consumer's taste-buds.

A word about so-called 'sauce mixes'. Notice that a line item in the ingredients reads: 'Enchilada Sauce Mix'. Usually I'm a hard liner when it comes to pre-packaged ingredients … I hate 'em. They're usually old as the hills when purchased and if you read the package ingredients closely, they sound more like components of a solid rocket booster than of something edible. But in cases such as Mexican, Asian and sometimes Italian cuisine, key ingredients are so scarce and difficult to balance properly that I throw in the towel and resign myself to using them. Just don't get in the habit of having some computer-driven machine determine what you will eat.

To make the tomato 'salsa' (sauce): Heat the olive oil (cold-pressed, extra-virgin) in a heavy-based saucepan over medium heat. Add the onions and garlic and sauté until the onions are transparent, approximately 4 minutes. Add the tomatoes, water, sauce mix and salt and pepper to taste.

Chicken Enchiladas continued

Bring to the boil, reduce the heat and simmer, stirring occasionally, until the sauce has reduced and thickened, approximately 15 minutes.

In a large bowl, combine the chicken, sour cream, chives and chilli powder. Season to taste with salt and pepper. Fine-tune the chilli powder to the LCD (lowest common denominator) of your group. In other words, make it up with Auntie Mabel in mind. Let your asbestos-throated brother-in-law jazz his up with a liberal sprinkling of jalapenos and a free hand with the tabasco. Remember: It's a breeze to make food hotter but you can't readily tone it down.

Preheat the oven to 180°C.

Deep-fry the tortillas, one at a time, until they have softened, about 30 seconds. Drain well on paper towels.

Divide the chicken mixture scientifically between the tortillas and roll 'em up. Place them seam side down in a baking dish. Pour the 'salsa' over them, scatter the olives over the top and sprinkle with the grated cheese. Bake in the oven for 15 to 20 minutes. Serve with crusty bread and a crisp green salad, or sliced tomatoes in oil, vinegar and some fresh cilantro. Serves 6 (not of Mexican descent).

INFORMAL ENTERTAINING*

(*Having guests over who
don't require you to wear shoes and socks.)

VEAL WITH MUSHROOMS AND PINEAPPLE

8 veal schnitzels

125 g field mushrooms, sliced

1 tablespoon butter

8 slices pineapple

125 mL cream

salt and freshly ground black pepper to taste

Here's veal with an Hawaiian twist! Veal schnitzels are fun to work with because they're tender, cook up in a jiffy and have a delicate, distinctive flavour. If you're like me and like your pineapple tart and flavourful rather than syrupy sweet, buy the type packed in its own juice rather than sugar. Better yet, buy it fresh and slice and core it just before cooking. You'll taste the difference immediately!

Season the veal with salt and pepper. Heat the butter in a heavy-based frying pan and when the butter foam subsides, fry the schnitzels on both sides until golden brown and cooked through, about 2–3 minutes per side. Gingerly remove from pan and keep warm.

Sauté the mushrooms in the same pan for 3 minutes, remove with a slotted spoon and keep warm. Place the pineapple slices into the pan and heat through; remove with the same slotted spoon and keep warm.

Pour the cream into the pan and deglaze by stirring the residue into the cream. Cook slowly, stirring until sauce thickens slightly.

On individual serving plates, arrange the veal slices, mushrooms and pineapple. Pour the sauce over and serve. Serves 8.

ROAST CHICKEN WITH HONEY AND PISTACHIO NUTS

1.5 kg roasting chicken

2 tablespoons honey

30 g unsalted butter

1 teaspoon rose water

30 g pistachio nuts, shelled
 and chopped

60 g *glacé* cherries, chopped

30 g preserved ginger,
 chopped

Here's a chicken recipe with definite Middle-Eastern overtones. Pistachios, in either their traditional red or trendy naturally coloured shells, have long enjoyed a prominent position in the snack nut hierarchy. It used to be that having red fingertips was a dead giveaway of pistachio possession to friends and foe alike. Undyed nuts changed all that. Now pistachio lovers can consume their stash undetected. As probably the final, unkindest cut of all, I've recently spied shelled pistachios for sale in clear plastic containers! Half the fun is shelling them! Next they'll sell them pre-digested …

The combination of the sweet honey and the sharp, nutty pistachios gives the roasting chicken amazing depth and character. Try this dish out on those friends who think they've had chicken every way imaginable. Chances are they'll rave about this new application of one of the world's favourite snacking nuts.

Preheat the oven to 180°C.

Melt the butter in a small saucepan and carefully add the honey. Stir well to combine. Using a sharp metal skewer, lance the entire breast and legs of the chicken. Rub some of the butter and honey mixture well into the flesh. Add the rose water to the remaining butter/honey mixture and pour inside the body cavity.

Place on a rack in a roasting tin and cook in the oven, basting with the pan juices from time to time, for approximately 1 hour or until the chicken is thoroughly cooked and tender.

Meanwhile, mix the nuts, cherries and ginger. As soon as the chicken is ready, carve into portions and sprinkle with the nut mixture. Serves 4.

LAZY MAN'S MEATLOAF

500 g premium mince beef

1 egg

1 slice bread, broken into
small pieces

1 medium onion, chopped

1 capsicum, cored,
deseeded and chopped

salt and pepper to taste

Don't think for a moment that I'm suggesting that 'Real Men' are shiftless, lazy sods. On the contrary, the two concepts are actually mutually exclusive. It's just that, speaking from bitter experience, often after a 15-hour stretch at the 'salt mines' preparing bullet-proof sales presentations, fending off unfriendly takeovers (corporate or otherwise!) or installing a new set of piston rings in a 1966 Jaguar XKE Cabriolet, the last thing we feel like doing is being boisterous and creative in the kitchen.

On those days when you find yourself praying for darkness, here's a hearty meatloaf you can sink your teeth into. It's also one of my few microwave dishes. And the best part of this meatloaf is you can reheat and reheat and reheat and reheat . . .

Combine all ingredients (as slapdash and carelessly as you like!) in a bowl and mix like hell. Scoop the mixture into a loaf-shaped, microwave-appropriate pan and cook on 'high' for 5 minutes (don't bother preheating the microwave!). Reduce setting to 'medium' and cook for a further 10 minutes. Let stand, undisturbed, for 5 minutes and serve with that natural accomplice, mashed potatoes, and the inevitable green vegetable. Serves 4.

PORK CHOPS WITH PRUNES

4 thick loin pork chops

440 g can prunes

250 mL dry white wine

1 tablespoon flour

1 tablespoon unsalted
   butter

1 tablespoon olive oil

125 mL cream

1 teaspoon redcurrant jelly

salt and freshly ground
   black pepper to taste

Long the brunt of countless jokes, the humble prune really shines here, providing excellent flavouring and a healthy dose of vitamins and minerals as well! Give this recipe a 'go' and I guarantee you'll have friends and family alike singing the praises of both you and the prune. Surely you don't mind sharing the spotlight!

Prunes and pork are not only great dinner partners, they're also both monosyllabic! The 'sleeper' ingredients here are the cream and redcurrant jelly …

Place prunes and wine in a saucepan and bring to the boil. Reduce the heat and simmer gently until the prunes are tender.

Place the flour on a flat plate and season with salt and pepper. Coat the chops in the flour. Heat the butter and the oil in a heavy-based frying pan. When the butter foam begins to subside, cook the chops on both sides until golden brown and cooked through, approximately 7–10 minutes each side. Remove from pan, place on absorbent kitchen paper and keep warm.

Drain the prunes and reserve the wine. Cook the remaining flour in the pan juices over medium heat for two minutes, being vigilant in preventing it from burning, which it naturally wants desperately to do.

Remove from the heat and gradually stir in the wine. When combined, return the pan to the heat and stir until the sauce thickens. Remove from the heat and add the cream and redcurrant jelly. Salt and pepper to taste.

Place the chops on individual serving dishes and deftly arrange prunes around them. Resist the temptation to create small sculptures with the prunes or to spell your guests' names in the piping hot fruit. The resulting comic effect is minimal. Serve with new potatoes, apple sauce or steamed mixed vegetables. Serves 4.

TAGLIATELLI (tahl-yah-telli) WITH BACON AND MUSHROOM SAUCE

750 g tagliatelli

250 g field mushrooms

6 rashers of bacon

1 tablespoon unsalted butter

125 g Parmesan cheese

2 tablespoons chopped parsley

salt and pepper to taste

This recipe calls for cooking the pasta until *al dente*. For the longest while, I grew up thinking this was a reference to an Italian relative. You know, Al Dente, son of Louis Dente, the construction contractor.

For some mysterious reason, many cooks insist on not only draining their pasta, but also rinsing the daylights out of it. This removes some surface starch, but also takes with it a good deal of flavour and texture. Next time you boil up some of this magical foodstuff, try draining it only. Guaranteed you'll be pleasantly surprised.

Wipe the mushrooms with a clean, damp cloth (NEVER WASH OR PEEL!), and slice. Chop the bacon into fine slices. Place 1 tablespoon of the butter into a heavy-based saucepan and fry the bacon for 3 minutes. Add the sliced mushrooms. Continue cooking, over medium heat, until the mushrooms are soft, approximately 2 minutes. Stir in the rest of the butter and parsley. Season to taste with salt and pepper.

Cook the tagliatelli in a large pan of boiling salted water, to which a dash of olive oil has been added. Cook until *al dente*, according to the directions on the packet. Drain the tagliatelli, then add the bacon and mushroom mixture and toss the pasta in it.

Place in a large serving dish and serve with Parmesan and more freshly ground black pepper, as desired. Serves 4–6.

FETTUCCINE (fet-uh-chee-nee) WITH TOMATOES AND ANCHOVIES

750 g fettuccine

1 tablespoon olive oil

100 g unsalted butter

1 onion, peeled and
 chopped

1 clove garlic, peeled and
 crushed

500 g tomatoes, peeled and
 chopped

6 anchovy fillets, chopped

120 g Parmesan cheese

1 tablespoon chopped basil

1 tablespoon chopped
 parsley

salt and freshly ground
 black pepper to taste

Pasta Power! I love pasta or, as my Italian friends call it, 'macaroni'. It's versatile, delicious, nutritious and so easy they've even had chimpanzees make it (under controlled circumstances) in several major zoos. White sauce, red sauce, olive oil and garlic – you name it! YOU CAN'T MISS! Here's a fettuccine recipe that'll have you swearing off the creamy Alfredo-type sauces forever …

To make the sauce: In a heavy-based saucepan, heat the olive oil and sauté the onion and garlic until the onion is transparent. Add the tomatoes, basil, anchovies, parsley and salt and pepper to taste. Bring to the boil, reduce heat and simmer gently for 30 minutes. Remove from the heat and strain through a fine sieve.

Cook the fettuccine in a large pan of boiling salted water to which a dash of olive oil has been added, according to the directions on the packet. Drain the fettuccine in a large sieve (DO NOT RINSE, just drain). Transfer to a large serving bowl and pour sauce over. Serve with grated Parmesan cheese on the side. Serves 4–6.

BRANDIED FILLET STEAK

4 fillet steaks, cut thick

1 clove garlic, peeled

150 g unsalted butter

20 mL brandy

4 sprigs of watercress

4 slices white bread, crusts
   removed

salt and freshly ground
   black pepper to taste

An impressive meal by anyone's measure, brandied fillet steak poses a real challenge to your creative juices. Use extra caution when cooking with brandy, especially on gas ranges, as it's the stuff that causes the fountains of fire with Cherries Jubilee and other spectacular flaming dishes.

(Tip: 'Real Men' always have a compact halon-type fire extinguisher handy in the kitchen. Not buried under tons of debris in a drawer or filed under 'miscellaneous' in the basement, but at hand in case of emergencies.)

Be a stickler for quality when purchasing your steak. Anyone who says you can't tell the difference hasn't been *cooking* with the brandy! For those particularly sensitive or susceptible to coronary arrest, delete the fried bread.

Place 60 g of the butter in a heavy-based frying pan and fry the bread on both sides until golden brown. Remove and keep warm.

Cut the garlic in half and rub over both sides of the fillet steaks. Season to taste with salt and pepper. Melt another 60 g of butter in yet another clean, heavy-based frying pan (what do you mean, you don't have two pans – start washing up, laddie!) and, when the butter foam subsides, fry the steak on both sides to your liking. Add the last 30 g butter and, when it has melted, pour the brandy over the steaks and *flambé*. Retain the brandy and butter mixture in the pan – it's the sauce!

Note: Roughly translated, *flambé* means to burn off the alcohol present in the brandy without burning off:
(a) your clothing
(b) substantial amounts of body/facial hair
(c) your kitchen cabinetry, or
(d) any other combustible materials in the vicinity.

Place one slice of fried bread on each serving plate and top with a fillet. Pour the brandy/butter sauce over, garnish with the watercress sprigs and serve with a mixed green salad. Serves 4.

Spanish Omelette

8 eggs

200 g cooked ham, finely sliced

1 small red capsicum, cored and deseeded

1 small green capsicum, cored and deseeded

3 large tomatoes, peeled and chopped

1 tablespoon olive oil

1 tablespoon unsalted butter

1 onion, peeled and finely chopped

1 small clove garlic, peeled and crushed

½ cup cooked peas

¼ teaspoon dried oregano

salt and freshly ground black pepper to taste

I've spent many a late evening, in many a New Jersey diner, contemplating the universe and the metaphysical significance of an abysmal cash flow, while eating Spanish omelettes on bullet-proof, industrial-strength dinnerware. They seem to make the perfect late-night meal, you know, in that twilight zone when it's much too late to be considered dinner and just a little too early to be considered breakfast. Spanish omelettes combine our friend the egg with hearty vegetables and seasonings. Mix and match with vegies, depending on your mood.

Break the eggs into a bowl and beat like a drum. Season to taste with salt and pepper. Chop the capsicums. Heat the oil and the butter in a heavy-based frying pan. When the butter foam subsides, sauté the onion and garlic until the onion is transparent. Add the capsicum and tomatoes and continue cooking for 3 minutes. Add the ham and peas. Stir well, in fact, stir better than well! Stir well enough to make your family, neighbours and countrymen proud! Stir so well that .. you get the idea.

Pour the beaten eggs evenly over the vegetables and cook without stirring until the eggs are set. Cut into wedges and serve with a crisp salad. Serves 4.

PRAWN RISOTTO

440 g can prawns

1 onion, peeled and finely chopped

1 clove garlic, peeled and crushed

1 tablespoon olive oil

440 g can sweetcorn kernels

2 cups rice

3 cups good chicken stock

1 cup dry white wine

1 tablespoon chopped parsley

salt and freshly ground black pepper to taste

125 g Parmesan cheese

Here's a culinary situation where bigger isn't necessarily better. Size may count in many instances in life (such as gridiron football), but when buying your prawns for risotto, buy no larger than medium-sized individuals

Those hefty critters that resemble lobsters with a thyroid condition just aren't suited to most cooking applications. Go for the small, sweet and tender instead. It's most discouraging to pan the room during the meal and see your guests jawing away on prawns that looked great in the fishmonger's shop, but bore a close textural resemblance to surgical tubing once they were prepared! Experiment with this dish by substituting different types of rice...

Place the oil in a large, heavy-based saucepan. Add the onion and garlic and sauté over medium heat until the onion is transparent. Add the rice and cook for 1 minute, stirring diligently so that the rice is well covered with the oil.

Add the stock and wine, bring to the boil, reduce the heat and simmer covered for 10 minutes. Add the drained prawns, sweetcorn and parsley. Season to taste with salt and pepper. Continue to cook gently until the rice is tender and all the liquid has been absorbed, approximately 10–15 minutes.

Place in a large serving dish. Serve with Parmesan cheese, crusty bread and crisp green salad. Serves 4.

STIR-FRIED STEAK

750 g rump steak, partially frozen

250 g snow peas

1 red capsicum, cored and deseeded

1 green capsicum, cored and deseeded

2 large carrots, scraped and diced

250 g mushrooms

125 g broccoli, cut into florets

2 zucchini, sliced

250 g can bamboo shoots

250 g can water chestnuts

1 onion, peeled and chopped

1 clove garlic, peeled and crushed

2 tablespoons olive oil

200 mL soy sauce

200 mL dry sherry

Some ersatz cooks think that just because they're stir-frying they can lean back in the steak department and get away with inferior meat. Not so! Have you ever watched dinner guests consume what was apparently industrial-grade polyurethane, mislabelled and sold at a supermarket as steak? It's one of those things you only do once. Splash out and start with good ingredients and you won't have to worry later. Stir-frying is quick, easy and nutritious. Grab your wok and let's go!

Slice the steak paper thin. In fact, slice it so it's suitable for use as cling wrap for leftovers! You'll find this much easier to do if the meat is partially frozen and the knife you're working with is razor sharp. Top and tail the snow peas and rinse them in cold running water. Pat dry with absorbent kitchen paper. Slice the capsicum. Wipe the mushrooms with a clean, damp cloth (NEVER, NEVER WASH OR PEEL) and slice. Drain the bamboo shoots and water chestnuts.

In a large wok, heat the oil over medium heat. Add the onion and garlic and sauté for 1 minute. Is anybody watching? If not, sneak in some extra garlic. Increase the heat, add the steak and vegetables and cook, stirring continuously, for 5 minutes. Add the soy sauce and the sherry and continue cooking for 2 minutes. Turn out onto a warmed serving dish, preferably in an Asian design, perhaps with a large blue goggle-eyed carp in an imaginary sea of white porcelain. Serve with boiled rice. Serves 6.

TUNA AND ONION VOL-AU-VENTS (vol-ah-vahnts)

4 medium vol-au-vent shells

2 small tins of tuna and onion

30 g butter

60 g flour

250 mL milk

15 g chopped parsley

salt and cracked pepper to taste

An excellent dish to spring on the linguistically uninitiated, or generally under-educated, since vol-au-vents can mean anything you want it to mean. Create some elaborate verbal ruse about the dish's murky French origins, including cryptic references to the Channel Islands, early Norman invasions of England and the nefarious Vichy-occupation government.

Be sure to know your audience beforehand, however, since one Rhodes Scholar could ruin your whole evening! Fortunately for us 'Real Men', most folks are so unknowledge-able regarding politics, world history and cooking, you'll have them eating out of the palm of your hand. But better to provide individual serving plates!

Pre-heat oven to 180°C. Place vol-au-vent shells in oven for 15 minutes.

Meanwhile, in your spare time, make a white sauce by melting the butter in a saucepan over a low heat and slowly stir in the flour with a wooden spoon (wooden spoons make the difference!). Gradually add the milk, stirring constantly until mixture is smooth and creamy.

Add tins of tuna and onion, parsley and salt and cracked pepper to taste. Fill the shells with the mixture and serve on a bed of rice. Serves 4.

QUICK SALMON PIE

500 g canned salmon

75 g rice

160 mL good chicken stock

1 onion, peeled and
   chopped

2 tablespoons butter

100 g button mushrooms

2 hard-boiled eggs,
   chopped

2 sheets of ready-rolled
   puff pastry

1 egg, beaten

2 tablespoons chopped
   parsley

salt and freshly ground
   black pepper to taste

This has nothing to do with formerly fast swimmers! It's a quick and easy way to prepare a tasty salmon dish for a party starter, main course or *après*-anything snack. Salmon is a miraculous fish, wonderfully red-fleshed and a game fighter on the end of a fishing rod. What better way to pay this noble protein source homage than by mastering a full repertoire of salmon recipes. This salmon pie is a sure hit!

Place the chicken stock and rice in a large saucepan. Add salt and pepper to taste. Bring to the boil, reduce heat and simmer until all the stock is absorbed and the rice tender. Add more stock if necessary to cook the rice fully.

Preheat the oven to 200°C.

Place the butter in a heavy-based saucepan and sauté the chopped onion until it's transparent, or at least painfully obvious. Wipe the mushrooms with a clean, damp cloth (Attention, mushroom washers and peelers: Mend your ways before it's too late!) and add them to the onions. Cook for two minutes.

Drain the salmon and, using a fork, flake the flesh. Combine the salmon, onions, mushrooms, cooked rice, boiled eggs and the chopped parsley in a large bowl. Season to taste with salt and pepper.

Grease a large baking tray. Grease it again, just for good measure! Place one sheet of the ready-rolled pastry (thank God for ready-rolled pastry!) on the baking tray. Spread the salmon filling onto this sheet, leaving about 2 cm all the way around.

Brush the border with some of the beaten egg. Place the second sheet of pastry over the filling and press the edges firmly together, artistically crimping with a fork. Brush the pie with the remaining beaten egg and bake in the oven for 30 minutes or until the pastry is golden brown and cooked thoroughly. Serve with buttered new potatoes and a green steamed vegetable. Serves 6.

Baked Avocado and Tuna

4 medium avocados, ripe

2 tins sandwich tuna

125 g grated Cheddar
  cheese

salt and grated black
  pepper to taste

4 sprigs of parsley

The perfect summertime treat that takes all of 10 minutes to prepare and that's in a strong headwind! Avocados are bristling with vitamins and minerals. (Why do you think those folks in Queensland look so trim, tanned and healthy all the time? Avocados. They eat zillions of 'em!). And the tuna's good for you too! If you're slimming, go light on the cheese or use cheese produced from low-fat milk, which is readily available in most supermarkets. A great dish when you can't be bothered being overly creative or resourceful …

Halve the avocados and remove the kernel. Fill the resulting hole with sandwich tuna. Cover each avocado with grated cheese and place under a hot grill until cheese browns, but doesn't burn, approximately 2–3 minutes. Serve with salt and pepper to taste, garnish with a sprig of parsley. Administer orally with ample cold beer! Serves 4.

SEAFOOD PANCAKES

4 eggs

600 mL milk

125 g flour, sifted

pinch salt

2 tablespoons light
vegetable oil

1 small carrot, scraped and
sliced

1 stalk celery, chopped

½ small onion, peeled and
finely chopped

3 tablespoons butter

2 tablespoons flour, extra

pinch cayenne pepper

150 g canned, peeled
prawns

150 g canned crabmeat

Here's an excellent 'power-brunching' dish that is nutritious, relatively easy to make and really creates the impression that you actually know what you're doing! Prawns and crabmeat are the seafood 'stars' of this show, so spend time and money buying excellent grades of each. Also, do your guests (and yourself) a favour and examine the crabmeat carefully for bits of cartilage and shell.

Place the flour (125 g) and salt into a large bowl. Add two of the eggs to 300 mL of the milk and beat well. Make a well in the centre of the flour and gradually add the egg/milk mixture and beat until smooth. Stir in the oil, cover the bowl with plastic wrap and refrigerate for 1 hour.

Place the remaining milk in a heavy-based saucepan and add the carrot, celery and onion. Bring to the boil, reduce heat and simmer for 2 minutes. Remove from the heat and set aside for 30 minutes, then strain.

Use this 30 minutes wisely. Do a crossword puzzle; read the first 10 pages of Joyce's *Ulysses*, concentrating on comprehension; conjugate several verbs in other than your native language;

Melt 1 tablespoon of butter in a heavy-based saucepan and add the extra flour. Stir well and cook over medium heat for 1 minute, being extra vigilant and not letting the flour burn. Remove from the heat and gradually stir in the strained milk. Return to the heat and cook, stirring continuously, until the sauce boils and thickens.

Separate the two remaining eggs. Melt the remaining butter in a saucepan, remove from the heat and add the beaten egg yolks. Season to taste with salt and pepper. Add to the sauce. Beat the egg whites until firm peaks form (this is also an excellent arm, wrist and elbow strengthening exercise!). Stir into the sauce along with the drained prawns and crabmeat.

Cook the pancakes one at a time on a large, greased, preheated frying pan or griddle and keep warm. Spoon filling onto each pancake and parcel them up, holding them together with toothpicks if necessary. Remind your guests several times to be mindful of the toothpicks! Enjoy! Serve with fresh fruit *compote*. Serves 6.

BACON AND CORN CHOWDER

4 rashers of bacon

1 tablespoon olive oil

1 large onion, peeled and
chopped

1 small clove garlic, peeled
and crushed

2 large potatoes, peeled
and sliced

350 mL good chicken stock

150 mL white wine

400 g diced ham

440 g can creamed corn

1 small can of evaporated
milk

1 tablespoon chopped
parsley

salt and freshly ground
black pepper to taste

Soups and chowders are perfect complements to lighter meals and are even terrific 'stand alone' dishes for quick snacks and lunches. Making the most basic soups is a snap, which is an excellent confidence builder for the culinary novice. They also score lots of bonus points in my kitchen since they can be heated and reheated numerous times with no loss of quality.

If you're single, living alone and make a normal-sized batch of soup (and have suffered no apparent ill effects after the first sampling), be sure to farm a lot of it out to friends and relatives. This strategy serves two purposes: (1) You just can't eat that much soup yourself; and (2) It will earn you 'good samaritan points' which may be redeemed at a later date. Try this bacon and corn chowder for real points-earning power…

Chop the bacon into small pieces. Heat the oil in a heavy-based saucepan and sauté the onion, garlic and bacon until the onion is transparent. Add the potatoes, chicken stock and wine. Bring to the boil, reduce heat and simmer, covered, for 10 minutes or until the potatoes are tender.

Remove from the heat and stir in the ham, creamed corn, evaporated milk and parsley. Season to taste with salt and freshly ground pepper. Return to the heat and continue to simmer, covered, for a further 3–4 minutes. Serve with hot buttered toast. Serves 6.

CHEESE AND HAM PIE

200 g cooked ham, finely
  sliced

200 g tasty Cheddar cheese,
  grated

1 small onion, peeled and
  chopped

1 tablespoon butter

2 sheets of ready-rolled
  puff pastry

1 egg

1 teaspoon French mustard

salt and freshly ground
  black pepper to taste

Good pies are terrific meals for several reasons. Executed properly, they look great, taste great and can be reheated endlessly! It has been reported that some small pubs in central Scotland and certain beach resorts on England's south coast are currently serving the last remaining slices of pies that were actually baked in the 1840s. And the patrons couldn't be happier! Reheating just makes 'em taste better. Feel free to experiment with ingredients and fine tune to your particular taste and mood …

Preheat the oven to 250°C.

Grease a large baking sheet and lay a sheet of the ready-rolled puff pastry on it (what did people do before ready-made pastry?). Spread the mustard over the pastry, leaving a border of 2 cm all around (get out those tape measures!).

Melt the butter in a heavy-based saucepan and sauté the onion until it is transparent. Spread the onion over the pastry sheet, still leaving the border clear (call in UN troops, if necessary!). Top with ham and then the cheese. Season with salt and pepper.

Place the egg in a bowl and beat well. Brush the edge of the pastry with the egg and place the second sheet of pastry over the first, pressing the edges together firmly. Brush the top of the pie with the remaining beaten egg and bake in the oven until golden brown, approximately 20–25 minutes. Serves 4.

STUFFED BAKED POTATOES

4 large potatoes

2 rashers of bacon

1 medium onion, chopped

250 mL sour cream

2 tablespoons chopped
  chives

125 g grated cheese

salt and pepper to taste

pinch of paprika

If stranded on a desert island and forced to select one food to have available in quantity, potatoes might get the nod. They're packed with nutrients, keep for ages and are very tasty! By baking potatoes and custom-blending different types of toppings and fillings, you can satisfy even the most pernickety palates. Here's where you can let your ingredient imagination run wild! I would, however, suggest you avoid fruit, whipped cream, anchovies, breakfast cereal and chocolate fudge sauce. They just don't seem to give the desired effect. My doctor will vouch for that!

Preheat the oven to 180°C.

Wash the potatoes carefully, scrubbing the skins with a soft, clean kitchen brush (don't use the one you reserve for bleaching your shirt collars – the potatoes will taste funny!). Grease the skins and bake in the oven for approximately 1 hour. Gingerly remove them from the oven (even 'Real Men' use dish towels or potholders!) and slice the broad side of the potato to provide enough of an opening to completely remove the interior contents. Put both the skins and contents aside and keep warm.

Cut the bacon into small bits and sauté in a heavy-based frying pan with the onion until onion is transparent.

In a bowl, combine the scooped out potato with the sour cream, bacon, onion, paprika and chives. Season to taste with salt and pepper and mix like your life depended on it! Fill the potato jackets with the mixture, sprinkle with grated cheese and bake in the oven for a further 10 minutes. Serve with a green salad and a glass or two of beer. Serves 4.

FORMAL ENTERTAINING

Individual Beef Wellington

4 fillet steaks

4 sheets of ready-rolled
  puff pastry

1 tablespoon butter

8 large field mushrooms,
  sliced

2 tablespoons sherry

salt and pepper to taste

1 egg

100 mL water

pinch of salt, extra

To use military parlance, here's a real 'launch-on-warning' dish that delivers 'ultimate force'. Beef Wellington is an almost apocryphal meal, one that's sure to score bonus points with even the most pernickety of palates. Most people have only heard of it, few have seen it and fewer still have actually ever had it. So even if yours isn't spot on, you still look like a hero.

Preheat the oven to 240°C.

Start by sharpening your scalpel and trim any visible fat and sinew from the steaks. Rinse each in cold water and pat dry with paper towelling. Heat the butter in a heavy-based frying pan and brown the steaks quickly on each side. Remember: they're being browned, not cooked for serving! Deftly remove the steaks from the pan, managing to avoid browning your fingers in the process.

Wipe the mushrooms with a clean, damp towel (never peel or wash!) and slice each once. Add them to the frying pan with the sherry and keep stirring until the mushrooms are tender (2–5 minutes).

Carefully lay out 4 sheets of puff pastry on a lightly floured bread board or work bench. In the middle of each square, place a mound of cooked mushrooms and a steak on top. Season to taste with salt and freshly ground black pepper. Fold each pastry sheet as if you were sending a parcel, consciously neglecting the cellotape and string. Place each parcel on a lightly greased baking sheet, folded side down. Mix the egg, water and pinch of salt together and brush the parcels with the mixture.

Transfer baking sheet to the heated oven and bake for 18–20 minutes, or until the pastry is golden brown. Best served with a hearty red wine and steamed vegetables. Serves 4, if at least one is slimming.

ROAST VEAL
WITH GARLIC AND ROSEMARY

1.5 kg shoulder of veal, boned

3 cloves garlic, peeled

1 teaspoon dried rosemary

salt and freshly ground black pepper

2 tablespoons olive oil

1 tablespoon butter

200 mL dry white wine

Garlic is a strategically significant element to virtually all cooking. The only meal for which I've been unable to find a successful garlic application is breakfast! Used judiciously, this odoriferous treat is one of the chief reasons for enduring the 'slings and arrows of outrageous fortune', to quote a long-dead pommy poet. However a word of warning is in order: try to consciously avoid garlic-packed meals around first dates, important sales presentations and public speaking engagements, as the tasty stuff can wreak havoc with your social/professional life.

Lay the veal on a flat, uncluttered work surface, skin side down. Slice the garlic and scatter over the meat, rubbing it in for good measure. Sprinkle the dried (use fresh-fresh-fresh if you can get it) rosemary over the meat. Roll up the meat and tie it securely and evenly with stout twine.

Heat the butter and oil in a heavy-based, flame-proof covered casserole (have several pot holders at the ready to work with the hot dishes). When the butter foam subsides, add the veal and quickly brown on all sides. Season to taste with salt and freshly ground black pepper. Add the wine and quickly bring back to the boil. Immediately reduce the heat to barely simmering. Place the lid on the casserole and cook very gently, turning occasionally, for 1½ to 2 hours, or until meat is very tender. Read the newspaper or some short stories. Do not, I repeat, do not start Thomas Mann's *The Magic Mountain*, or Proust's *Remembrance of Things Past*. If the cooking liquid begins to evaporate, add a little warm water (not cold water!).

When tender, remove veal from casserole and set aside to rest in a warm place. Rekindle the flame under the casserole and reduce gravy by boiling. Expertly carve the veal and place on your most flamboyant serving dish, you know, that neo-rococo horror you picked up at a garage sale for two dollars. The one trimmed with gilt grapes and resplendent with dead waterfowl. Drizzle the gravy over the meat and serve. Accompany this dish with boiled potatoes, snow peas and yellow baby squash. Serves 8 (confirmed veal eaters).

STIR-FRY PORK WITH CASHEWS

750 g pork fillet, partially frozen

75 g unsalted cashew nuts, coarsely chopped

1 clove garlic, peeled and crushed

2 tablespoons olive oil

2 tablespoons soy sauce

1 dash tabasco sauce

freshly ground black pepper

Asian cooking requires an inventive flair, a free hand with the Hoi-sin sauce and lightning-like reflexes. If your attempt falls miserably short, don't despair! Do what I do: keep your dripping pots and dishes cluttered about the stove, call your nearest Chinese takeaway (preferably one that delivers) and plop down in front of the telly until your emergency order arrives. Bury the containers in the garbage, transfer the contents to your pots and cover until your guests arrive. As the doorbell rings, crank up the heat under your bogus creations, sit back and soak up the praise at the table. The next day, send your Chinese place an anonymous 'Thank You' note. This chases away any evil spirits antagonised by your culinary hi-jinks.

Finely slice the pork fillet (this is much easier when the meat is partially frozen). Heat the oil in a wok (first choice) or a heavy-based frying pan (poor second) over medium heat. Add the pork and stir-fry for approximately 2–3 minutes (no pork sushi please!). Add remaining ingredients and stir copiously, cooking the mixture until the pork is tender (approx. 5–7 minutes). Serve immediately with plain boiled rice. Keep the tabasco bottle at the ready and fine-tune your plate at will. Stir-fried food has an extraordinarily narrow 'window of opportunity' for optimal taste and texture. Try not to dilly-dally while serving. Encourage your guests to eat at once. Serves 4 (who've eaten at least once during the last six hours).

BEEF STROGANOFF

750 g fillet steak, partially
frozen

500 g mushrooms

1 medium onion, peeled
and sliced

4 tablespoons butter

150 mL good beef stock

2 tablespoons tomato purée

¼ teaspoon mixed herbs

salt and pepper to taste

300 mL light sour cream

The legendary dish from imperial Russia. Who said those pre-Bolsheviki weren't a lot of fun! Drink a short vodka (always keep your vodka in the freezer) toast to 'Glasnost' and 'Perestroika' before embarking on this very tasty meal.

Finely slice the fillet steak. If you can't comfortably read the evening paper through it, it's too thick! This task is easier to do when the meat is slightly frozen. Wipe the mushrooms with your ever-present clean, damp cloth and carefully slice them.

Melt the butter in a heavy-based frying pan. Add the meat and stir-fry quickly until brown. Remove the meat from the pan with a slotted spoon and keep warm. Add the mushrooms and onions to the pan and sauté gently until the onions are tender and transparent.

Return the steak to the pan and add the beef stock, tomato purée, mixed herbs. Season to taste with salt and pepper. Add the sour cream and bring to the boil, stirring vigilantly. Let this mixture stick and you're in 'deep Vegemite'! Reduce the heat dramatically and simmer until the meat is tender, usually in about 5–7 minutes.

In a separate pot boil up the best wide egg noodles you can get your hands on, following the instructions from your noodle purveyor, or if you must, the package they came in. Don't buy dodgy noodles to save a few pennies – they generally taste like cardboard. If you can buy fresh pasta, by all means do! And never rinse 'em, it washes all the good stuff away. Serve with a tossed green salad. Serves 4 (with a tail-wind, serves 4.5 adults. Insist that the .5 adult do the washing up).

NOISETTES (nwah-setz) OF LAMB WITH HERB BUTTER

500 g loin of lamb, boned

2 tablespoons butter

1 tablespoon olive oil

salt and pepper to taste

1 clove garlic, peeled
and crushed

Herb Butter
1 tablespoon butter

½ tablespoon chopped
fresh thyme

½ tablespoon chopped
fresh parsley

The real question is, ''Where are the noisettes on a lamb?'' If you answered just behind the shoulder blade, you're in big trouble. On second thought, if you even asked the question you should probably use this book to start a campfire! If you like lamb like I do, and I love it, here's a dish that will turn a lot of heads at your dining table. Lamb has a delicate flavour and should be herbed and spiced very delicately. The only acceptable applications for heavily spiced lamb usually appear in certain Middle Eastern and Afghani dishes and this is primarily a function of the often hazy heritage or pedigree of available meat.

Trim off all the outer skin of the lamb and all visible fat. Spread the loin out on a flat, uncluttered working surface and sprinkle with seasoned salt, freshly ground pepper and a hint of garlic (different people have different-sized hints, much like noisettes). Roll up and tie securely and evenly with string at 3 cm intervals. Then neatly cut the roll (between the string) into 4 noisettes.

To make the herb butter: Soften the butter and place in a bowl. Add the chopped herbs (use fresh-fresh-fresh) and mix well. Scoop out the butter and place on a piece of greaseproof paper and roll up to form a log. Chill in the refrigerator until firm.

Heat the oil and the butter in a heavy-based frying pan and when the butter foam subsides, add the noisettes and cook on each side for approximately 5 minutes or until lamb is cooked to your liking. Lamb, like fish, should not be overcooked.

Arrange 2 noisettes on each dinner plate. Remove the string (or serve with the string if you're trying to create an atmosphere of total incompetence). Top each noisette with a slim slice of herb butter and serve with baby new potatoes, steamed julienne of carrots and snow peas. Serves 2 (keep a sharp eye on your plate!).

LEMON ROAST PORK

1.5 kg loin of pork, boned
and rolled

1 teaspoon salt

Grated rind of 2 lemons

1 teaspoon fresh
chopped sage

Preheat the oven to 220°C.

A 'low-tech' pork dish and all-round favourite for anytime eating. Present this dish with a multitude of mix'n'match vegies, or a tossed green salad and mashed potatoes. Fire up the oven!

Industriously score the rind of the pork. Rub the salt, lemon rind and sage well into the skin. Place the pork on a roasting rack in a foil-lined baking tin and roast in the oven for approximately 20 minutes. Reduce your heat to 180°C and cook for a further 2 to 2½ hours or until the pork is cooked and the juices run clear when pierced with a skewer.

Remove from the oven and allow to stand for 10 minutes before carving. Garnish with lemon slices and serve with apple sauce, roast potatoes, red cabbage and zucchini. Serves 8 (6 if they're all a bit peckish).

ROAST JUMBUCK (lamb)

1 leg of lamb, approx. 2.5 kg

3 cloves of garlic

12 fresh sprigs of rosemary
  or 1 teaspoon of dried

30 g plain flour

1 teaspoon paprika

salt and black pepper
  to taste

Preheat the oven to 180°C.

Now there's a sweepstakes winner for you, 'Jumbuck'. Sounds faintly South African, or perhaps Caribbean – let alone Australian. Also sounds like a sporty automobile: "The assailant left the scene in a hail of bullets, speeding away in a cream-coloured, late-model Jumbuck convertible." If you're hard-pressed to find any Jumbucks in your supermarket meat department, don't despair, lamb will do very nicely!

Peel the garlic and cut into thick slices. With a sharp knife (the only kind 'Real Men' use!), make a few deep surgical incisions in the leg of lamb (operating gowns not required!). Insert a slice of garlic and a pinch of rosemary in each incision. Combine the flour, paprika, salt and pepper in a small bowl. Rub this mixture liberally into the skin of the roast.

Stand the lamb on a rack in a roasting tin. Place in the oven and roast for 20 minutes per 500 g, plus 20 minutes extra for good measure. Remove from the oven and allow to rest before carving. Serve with mint sauce, roast potatoes, baked butternut pumpkin and peas. Serves 8 (or 4 after a full day's fishing).

SPECIAL PEPPER STEAK

4 fillet steaks, approx.
  200 g each

1 tablespoon cracked black
  pepper

60 g unsalted butter

2 tablespoons olive oil

1 clove garlic, peeled

salt to taste

125 mL sweet sherry

125 mL good beef stock

60 mL double cream

Many people ask me, "What's so special about pepper steak?" Well, you've got to try it to know! I can't over-emphasise the importance of starting this dish with good, fresh cracked pepper. The stuff you keep on the shelf is usually not fit for consumption. Think about it – how long has it been there? Six months, a year, two years? The way most people use peppercorns, a 175 g tin virtually lasts a lifetime. Buy some new black peppercorns at a gourmet shop, or completely lose your grip and buy some pink or multi-coloured peppercorns and give them a go. Unlike heat-seeking missiles, they're neither dangerous nor expensive. So go ahead, experiment!

Sprinkle the cracked peppercorns onto each side of the steak, pressing them well into the meat. Place the butter, the olive oil (use cold-pressed, extra-virgin oil only!) and garlic clove in a heavy-based frying pan and combine over medium–high heat. When the foam subsides, remove garlic and add the steaks to sear both sides evenly. Reduce to medium heat and cook steaks to your and your guests' taste. Remove the steaks from the pan and keep warm until ready to serve. Remove the pan from the heat and pour off the lion's share of the fat, retaining approximately 1 tablespoon. Pour in the sherry and stock, deglazing the pan juices by scraping the residue into the wine/stock mixture. Replace the pan to the heat and bring to the boil, stirring copiously. Cease stirring but continue to boil until sauce reduces to a quarter of its original volume.

Remove pan from the heat and add the cream, stirring until combined. Place back over a low heat and stir until sauce reheats (but doesn't boil).

Place each steak on a serving plate, spooning the sauce over them. Serve with plain boiled potatoes, broccoli and baby carrots. Serves 4 (more or less).

Pork Stuffed with Apricots and Apples

1.5 kg loin of pork, boned with skin well scored

100 g ready-to-eat dried apricots

salt and pepper to taste

2 apples

2 tablespoons olive oil

30 g unsalted butter

175 mL white wine

175 mL single cream

180 mL water

2 teaspoons redcurrant jelly

1 teaspoon French mustard

3 teaspoons cornflour

60 mL water, extra

Preheat the oven to 230°C.

Combining these popular fruits with pork makes this recipe a tried-and-true favourite. Once you get the hang of it, try different kinds of fruit and sincerely try to look humble amidst showering praise and rave reviews in the kitchen!

Lay the pork out flat (preferably using a 'right cross' or a 'left-right combination'), meat side up. If the meat refuses to lie flat, release a lot of aggression through the strident use of a meat mallet. Think of that meeting where Mallory made you look like a turkey in front of the CEO! Think of that time your car's windscreen wipers quit in the middle of a driving rainstorm! Think of military defence contract fraud! Think of inhumane foreign policy!

If the meat still refuses to lie flat, ask if you can be its agent for a light–heavyweight title bout in Las Vegas and cook something else! Season with salt and pepper to taste.

Peel, core and slice the apples. Arrange the (pitted!) apricots and apple slices over the pork and roll up firmly. Tie the meat securely at even intervals along the roast. Rub salt and freshly ground pepper over the skin. Place the pork on a rack in a roasting tin and cook in the oven, allowing 35 minutes per 500 g and 35 minutes extra. Cook for the first 30 minutes at 230°C, then turn the oven down to 180°C for the remaining cooking time. Baste frequently with pan drippings.

Remove roast from the oven and set aside in a warm place to rest while you create your magical sauce. Pour all the fat from the roasting pan. Pour in the wine (reserving a bit for inspiration) and deglaze the pan by scraping the residue into the mixture. Pour this into a clean saucepan. Add the cream, water, redcurrant jelly and mustard. Place the pan over medium heat and bring to the boil. Mix the cornflour and extra water together until smooth. Add to the sauce, stirring constantly. Cook until sauce boils and thickens. Season to taste with salt and pepper.

Slice the pork and serve with sauce spooned over it. Serve with steamed red cabbage and whole baby squash. Serves 8 (6 if 2 have just been rescued at sea).

SPECIAL LEMON CHICKEN

6 large chicken fillets

40 mL white wine

juice of 1 lemon

½ teaspoon dried thyme

salt and pepper to taste

1 red capsicum

1 green capsicum

250 g button mushrooms

2.5 cm piece of fresh ginger

Next to fish, chicken is my favourite flesh! It's so versatile and can be presented in so many tasty ways. It's a safe bet to serve with all but the hard-core plantarian set. As always, marinating is important here and should be attended to accordingly. Combining the flavours of the lemon and capsicum, this is one chicken dish that won't trouble you with leftovers.

Combine the wine, lemon juice, thyme and seasoning in a small bowl. Slice the chicken fillets into bite-sized strips (mind those mouths!). Marinate the chicken in the wine mixture for at least 1 hour (more like 2–3 hours or overnight!).

Wash, core and de-seed the capsicum, cutting it into small (1.5 cm) strips (get out your calipers!). Wipe the mushrooms with a clean damp cloth. Place the chicken and capsicum into a steaming basket and steam for 4 minutes. Add the button mushrooms and continue to steam for an additional 4 minutes until the chicken is cooked.

Meanwhile, in your spare time, peel and grate the ginger. Place in a piece of clean cloth. Place the chicken and vegetables in a warm serving bowl. Twist the ends of the cloth bearing the ginger to squeeze ginger juice over the chicken and vegetables. Serve with plain boiled rice and sliced tropical fruit. Serves 6 (or thereabouts).

BEEF AND VEGETABLE STIR-FRY

500 g rump steak

2 tablespoons light
  soy sauce

2 tablespoons sherry

4 tablespoons olive oil

2 cloves garlic, peeled
  and crushed

2 teaspoons shredded fresh
  ginger root

2 celery stalks, chopped

2 onions, peeled and cut
  into quarters

200 g can bamboo shoots,
  drained

200 g can water chestnuts,
  drained and sliced

Flash stir-frying, over high heat, is an excellent way to prepare dishes that are both healthful and satisfying. Ingredients are cut into small pieces to ensure even, uniform cooking. Meats are usually given a head start by cooking them first and adding the vegetables later, for an even briefer cooking time. Do yourself a favour and get set up with a proper Asian wok and utensils. Follow the instructions carefully regarding 'seasoning' the wok and after-cooking care. Stir-frying without a wok is not unlike beating a rattlesnake to death with a pair of pantihose – it can be done, but the results are likely to be noticeably inferior.

Chill the rump steak, making it easier to slice. Cut into thin slices. (Each slice should be able to fit neatly into your computer's floppy disk drive. While performing this test, do not attempt to 'boot up' under any circumstances!) Mix the soy sauce and sherry (a popular age-old ingredient in many Asian recipes!) and marinate the meat in this mixture for at least 1 hour (2–3 hours is preferable).

Heat the oil in a wok over a high heat. Add the garlic and ginger and stir-fry for about 1 minute. Add the celery and onions and stir-fry for 2 minutes. Add the bamboo shoots and water chestnuts and continue cooking for 1 minute. Remove the vegetables with a slotted spoon and keep warm.

Remove the beef from the marinade, reserving the marinade. Add the beef to the wok and stir-fry for 45 seconds or until cooked. Add the marinade and toss the beef well in this mixture. Add the beef to the vegetables and toss together. Place in a serving dish and serve promptly with boiled rice or thin Asian noodles. Serves 6 (depending on their appetites!).

VEAL CORDON BLEU
(kor-done bluh)

4 veal steaks, approx. 125 g
   each

4 slices leg ham

2 eggs, lightly beaten

30 g flour, seasoned with
   salt and freshly ground
   black pepper

125 g Gruyère cheese

fine breadcrumbs
   for coating

125 mL olive oil

2 tablespoons butter

A 'blue-ribbon' winner of veal dishes that will not only win you laurels with friends, relatives or that 'significant other' in your life, but also provides an excellent therapeutic aggression release via the meat mallet. A word of warning: When many recipe instructions and cuts of meat were invented, stress and frustration levels were nowhere near the dizzying heights they've achieved in modern 'civilised' society. As a result, the use of a meat mallet in this regard should be governed by a judicious eye to the meat, ensuring that your pent-up, vitriolic rage doesn't reduce a pricey cut of veal to stringy tatters. If you're feeling particularly close to the edge, go work out at the health club, split some firewood or participate in a triathlon. Then come back and hoist the pots and pans. Your subsequently created meals will positively reflect your stabilised psyche.

Using a meat mallet (don't be tempted to grab that framing hammer from your workbench), pound the steaks until they're approximately 4 mm thick. Spread them out flat on a clean, uncluttered work surface and brush the upper side with the beaten egg. Also dust that side with seasoned flour.

Divide the cheese into four equivalent portions. Mate each portion with a slice of ham and roll up. Place the ham roll onto the floured side of the veal and fold the veal steak over, encasing the ham. Press firmly around the edges to seal. Coat each piece of veal with more seasoned flour and dip into the beaten egg. Then coat with fine breadcrumbs. Place on a flat plate and cover with a dish or plastic wrap. Refrigerate for approximately 1 hour.

Heat the oil and butter in a heavy-based frying pan. When the butter foam subsides, add the veal carefully and cook over a medium heat for about 7 minutes each side. Remove from the pan and drain on paper towels. Serve garnished with lime wedges and a crisp Italian salad. Serves 4 (moderately hungry adult humans).

HERBED RACKS OF LAMB

2 racks of lamb, consisting of 6 chops each

Marinade
2 tablespoons olive oil

juice of 1 lemon

salt and freshly ground black pepper to taste

2 cloves garlic, peeled and crushed

¼ teaspoon fresh chopped thyme

¼ teaspoon fresh chopped rosemary

¼ teaspoon fresh chopped parsley

A visual show-stopper, herbed racks of lamb are absolutely winners when presentation counts. For the real clincher, decorate the ends of the chops with those tiny sliced paper caps. I've no idea what purpose they serve or where they came from, but every cookbook photo I've ever seen of racks of lamb has them prominently featured. With these and similar inedible, mystifying culinary traditions, I often muse that someone, somewhere, had to do that for the first time. Imagine what his guests must've said, having never seen paper rack caps in any cookbook before! The mind boggles. The chef was probably hanged for his innovation.

Score the back of the lamb racks with light diagonal cuts. Place in a large, flat dish. Combine the ingredients for the marinade and brush the racks of lamb well with the mixture. Cover the dish and marinate for at least 2 hours, occasionally brushing the lamb with more marinade.

Preheat the oven to 190°C. Place the lamb on a roasting rack in a baking tin. Baste with some more of the marinade and roast in the oven for 45 minutes or until the lamb is cooked to your liking.

Remove and let stand for about 5 minutes before carving, 2 cutlets per person. Serve with minted new potatoes, baked pumpkin and peas. Serves 6 (or 5 adults and 2 boisterous, fidgety children).

Veal Escalopes (Eska-lopes) with Fennel (Fenl)

4 veal escalopes

2 tablespoons butter

30 g flour, seasoned with salt and freshly ground black pepper

3 tablespoons chopped shallots

½ cup finely chopped fennel leaves

juice of 1 lemon

salt and pepper to taste

For you fans of escalopes out there (and their socio-cultural equivalents around the world), here's another veal dish that not only works, but doesn't even take five minutes for a coffee break! The distinctive flavour of fennel provides an interesting counterpoint to the delicate taste and texture of the veal. In order to maximise positive response I suggest polling your audience ahead of time as to their feelings about fennel. Some folks like it, some don't. Again, knowing your consumer audience will allow you to achieve peak product acceptance!

Dust the veal with the seasoned flour. Heat the butter in a heavy-based frying pan and quickly brown the veal on both sides. Add the shallots, cover the pan, reduce the heat and simmer for around 5 minutes. Stir in the fennel, lemon juice, salt and pepper. Cook for 1 minute more and serve immediately, accompanied by steamed mixed vegetables or a tossed green salad. Serves 4 (give or take).

CARPET-BAG STEAK

4 fillet steaks

300 g unsalted butter

18 oysters

250 g mushrooms

1 tablespoon chopped
  parsley

170 g fine breadcrumbs

zest of 1 lemon

salt to taste

paprika to taste

1 egg

Following the conclusion of the American Civil War, proto-entrepreneurs from the victorious industrial North descended like locusts on the ravaged agricultural South. With the land, people and local economy in ruins (fortunately for the Northerners most of the warfare took place in the South!), these magnanimous fellows came carrying hard currency, buying everything in sight from its destitute owners for a tiny fraction of what it was really worth.

This barbaric behaviour earned them the nickname 'Carpet-baggers', since they usually appeared at what was left of the local train station toting oversized hand luggage that was constructed of heavy fabric, printed or woven in garish designs and patterns, much like the carpeting of the day. This example of capitalism at its worst (best?) plunged the reeling South into nearly complete economic and social collapse and inflicted a wound so deep in US society that vestiges of bitterness and hate still exist today. But how does this relate to a steak recipe…?

Heat half the butter in a heavy-based frying pan and toss the mushrooms and oysters in it for approximately 2 minutes. Transfer to a bowl and add the breadcrumbs, parsley, lemon zest and seasonings. Add the beaten egg and combine well.

With a very sharp knife (the only kind!), carefully cut a pocket in the side of each fillet steak and fill it with the stuffing created above (for those interested, this is the 'carpet bag' part). Close the opening with one or two toothpicks.

Heat the remaining butter in the pan and cook the steaks to your liking. Don't cook the life out of them – these are good steaks! Serve with roast potatoes and pumpkin. Serves 4 (or 9, if 5 are only having wine and cigars).

FILLETS OF LAMB WITH PORT

1 kg lamb fillets

350 mL good red wine

175 mL port

3 tablespoons cornflour

salt and freshly ground
   black pepper

1 teaspoon fresh, chopped
   rosemary

2 tablespoons unsalted
   butter

1 teaspoon sugar

1 tablespoon French mustard

2 cloves garlic, crushed

OK! OK! I admit it! Lamb is a personal favourite. It's so versatile, uniquely yet delicately flavoured and so universally popular that in my book it's hard to beat for taste, nutrition and real meal value. Adding the tangy sweetness of port gives the fillets an extra dimension that I know you and your guests will love. Try this dish in a special 'strategic' situation and I'm sure you'll be pleased with the results.

According to an ancient Macedonian legend, combining the above ingredients occasionally produces an unexplainably intense reaction which is nearly impossible to counteract. Unfortunately the ravages of time have hopelessly blurred the key word concerning the type of reaction from the stone tablets bearing this legend. Some scholars feel it says 'aphrodisiac', while others say it resembles a word for 'pyrotechnic flatulence'. Good luck!

Sprinkle 1 tablespoon of the cornflour onto a large plate and season with the salt, pepper and rosemary. Coat the lamb fillets with this mixture.

Heat the butter in a heavy-based frying pan. When the foam subsides brown the fillets on both sides. Reduce the heat and cook the fillets to your liking, usually no more than 5–7 minutes. Remember, lamb is especially prone to over-cooking since it's so delicate. Avoid lamb sushi but mind the overcooking as well. Remove the lamb from the pan and reserve in a warm place.

Mix the remaining cornflour with a little of the red wine to create a smooth paste and add to the pan with the remaining wine, port, sugar, mustard and garlic. Bring to the boil, reduce heat and simmer until the sauce thickens. Special note: Watch your sauces like a hawk! They have one of the narrowest 'windows of palatability' in all cooking. Stir diligently and keep the heat low, don't boil 'em.

Slice the fillets, arrange on serving plates and pour the sauce over them. Serves 8 (or 5 'Real Lamb Eaters').

DIJON PORK CHOPS

4 large pork chops

2 tablespoons grated
  Gruyère cheese

2 tablespoons Dijon mustard

2 tablespoons light cream

1 red capsicum, cored,
  de-seeded and sliced

1 green capsicum, cored,
  de-seeded and sliced

salt and pepper to taste

Preheat the oven to 190°C.

Pork chops are hearty fare, usually serving as stalwarts in the 'Real Man's' repast repertoire. When the phrase 'meat and potatoes' was coined to connote a diet as well as a psychic lifestyle, pork chops are probably what they had in mind. Here's a way to perk them up with one of the earth's more urban delights: Dijon mustard.

Place the cheese and mustard in a bowl and mix like hell. Add the cream and salt and pepper to taste. Place a quarter of this mixture on each chop.

Place the chops in a warmed baking dish, big enough to accommodate them in a single layer. Arrange the capsicum strips over and around the chops and cover the dish with aluminium foil. Place in the oven and bake for 45 minutes or until the chops are thoroughly cooked. Serve with steamed red cabbage, mashed potatoes and baby green beans. Serves 4 (depending on appetites).

PORK STEAKS WITH MADEIRA SAUCE

4 large pork leg steaks

1 clove garlic, peeled

300 mL dry white wine

½ tablespoon white wine vinegar

1 bay leaf

1 glass Madeira

salt and freshly ground black pepper

handful of plump raisins

Preheat the oven to 190°C.

Cooking with wine is a natural. You can assure your maiden aunties that they are perfectly safe consuming your drink-doused dish because the cooking heat evaporates all the alcohol before the meal is served. Yet the subtle flavouring remains to complement nearly every main ingredient. It also allows the cook to temper the sometimes hectic pace in the kitchen with an intermittent nip of grape. I'm not a big believer in hard liquor in the kitchen, except for a few remote exceptions (see Chilli and Ribs), for two major reasons.

First and foremost, an open bottle of anything with an alcohol content or 'proof' higher than the average human IQ poses a real fire hazard near the stove. And secondly because, contrary to popular notion, getting hammered in the kitchen doesn't do your cooking any good! Anyone who tells you they can cook, write, make love, paint or play music better when they're under the influence of ANY drug are either: (a) currently drunk; (b) a chronic substance abuser; (c) almost completely stupid; or (d) any combination of the above.

So go buy some splendid pork, break out the Madeira and let's go…

Rub the pork steaks with the garlic cloves and place them in a shallow, flame-proof dish. Gently add the wine and the vinegar. Note: The liquid should just cover the steaks – if it doesn't, add just enough warm (not cold!) water to bring it up to snuff.

Cover the dish and carefully place in your oven for approximately 1 hour. Place the steaks on a warm serving dish and keep warm while you make the sauce. Pour the pan juices into a clean saucepan and add the Madeira (in the interest of strict quality control, sample before adding!). Bring to the boil, reduce the heat, add a handful of plump raisins and simmer for 2 to 3 minutes. Pour sauce over the meat and serve immediately, garnished with slices of cooked apple. Accompany with steamed peas and carrots. Serves 4 (for the most part).

VEAL NORMANDE (nor-mahnd)

4 veal schnitzels

1 clove garlic, peeled and crushed

250 g field mushrooms, sliced

2 onions, peeled and sliced

3 tablespoons butter

600 mL light cream

1 teaspoon mixed herbs

60 mL brandy

90 mL dry white wine

A memorable meal for fans of veal. I encourage market research to determine your dinner guests' outlook on veal. More than half the battle of marketing is knowing your target market inside and out. The product is inconsequential. If veal is right for you and yours, this preparation more than does it justice.

Melt half the butter in a heavy-based frying pan, adding the garlic, mushrooms (you didn't wash those mushrooms, did you?) and onion. Sauté gently until the onion is soft and transparent. Gently add the cream, herbs, brandy and wine. Simmer gently until the sauce reduces and thickens. Keep a close watch on the sauce as it reduces, avoid burnouts that require pneumatic equipment for the washing up!

In a separate frying pan, heat the remaining butter and sauté the veal schnitzels over a medium heat until tender. Pour the sauce over the veal and allow to heat through. Serve with steamed potatoes, broccoli and baby carrots. Some crusty French bread would be a nice addition! Serves 4 (or so).